SOUL MATE CONNECTIONS

Everything You Ever Wanted To Know About Relationships, Love, Romance and Soul Mates

Myrna Lou Goldbaum
Palmist

SOUL MATE CONNECTIONS

Everything You Ever Wanted To Know About Relationships, Love, Romance and Soul Mates

TO:
Joyce

1/5/11

Hope you like this book.

Myrna Lou
Goldbaum

ISBN 0-7414-1409-0

Published by:

INFINITY
PUBLISHING.COM

519 West Lancaster Avenue
Haverford, PA 19041-1413
Info@buybooksontheweb.com
www.buybooksontheweb.com
Toll-free (877) BUY BOOK
Local Phone (610) 520-2500
Fax (610) 519-0261

Printed in the United States of America

Printed on Recycled Paper

Published February 2003

DEDICATION

I dedicate this book to all those whose palms I have read in the past 53 years who I ascertained were either with their soul mates or seeking them. I have danced at many weddings of those whose hands I have read where I predicted a union would take place.

It is my hope that the readers learn about their relationships and see their own life dilemmas in one of the stories presented here. Advice given to those in palm reading sessions may prove beneficial.

In soul mate relationships change is what makes the world move. Change and development are necessary to facilitate growth. In any relationship, be it male-female, mother-daughter, sisters, or two male friends, changes are in their lives. Because love and romance cause the world to turn, movement is good if it is towards a goal and not away from it.

Table of Contents

SOUL MATE CONNECTIONS

INTRODUCTION:

Most individuals believe they know and understand the term "soul mate", but if asked to define it they transmit fuzzy meanings that do not convey the true essence of soul mate. The definition of a SOUL MATE: one who bonds with another, instantly familiar with them, as if they are created as one; two minds working in tandem. It is as if they are a single unit, nurturing, bonding and loving. Soul mates constantly search for their equal. They connect on a soul level and feel what the other is experiencing simultaneously. Soul mates have "agreements" established in a previous karmic past to share their evolutionary growth. Having had experiences with that individual in a previous lifetime causes sparks when they reunite. An open, carefree attitude and creativity are present where risk-taking aids in the acceptance of the individual. Both people in the relationship experience spontaneity, fresh ideas and change. The relationship is assumed to remain in existence forever.

Wisdom in life situations is not found in books but attained only through living life and having experiences. The inner travel of the soul is a gift we give ourselves. When we get in touch with our higher self, feel our soul and understand a sense of what gives us true happiness, the discovery of old worn-out patterns can be realized. Releasing old patterns allows new and healthier ones to emerge.

The admission to self, "I want my other half, my true soul mate" is sent out into the universe. A soul mate reads the signal as a gut-wrenching cry for him or her and answers the "call" home.

Being in touch with one's higher self and connecting to one's scared self are the real benefits of palmistry. The

1

lines on a human palm are the indicators of the major influences and movements one faces in life. The human hand is considered the mirror of the soul. The hand is also the servant of the human brain. Palmistry searches for the truth that enables knowing the true nature of another.

PALMISTRY ADDRESSES THE ISSUES OF:

Relationships, family, friendships, love, soul mate, emotional turmoil, dreams, ambition, future goals and creating work that gives one's heart joy. Palmistry helps one find his or her spiritual path and creates more meaning to build a more fulfilling life.

Everyone should carefully observe which way his heart draws him and then choose that way with all his strength."

Chassidic Proverb

RELATIONSHIPS

The greatest relationship is the one that we have with ourselves for that determines the quality of the relationship we have with others. The basic purpose of a relationship is to provide mutual support for each other. The ability to provide this kind of nurturing support to someone other than self is a precious gift. The basis of any relationship requires respect, autonomy and mystery. Any relationship can be a spiritual path toward enlightenment, however it must be built on truthful communication where neither person feels superior all the time. In a solid, successful soul mate relationship the leadership shifts back and forth between the couple, where sometimes one partner is in control and has all the bright ideas and their partner goes with the flow. The next day the creative ideas may flow and develop from the other person. Neither partner is always the leader or the follower.

When a person knows the type of partner they seek in a mate and seriously contemplates discovering that person, they are bound to discover what is rightfully theirs. Relationships are not simply a project to be taken on. Humans are not used to dealing with grace artfully, appreciating one another and giving thanks, honoring and celebrating life. A relationship is not in existence to make us feel good inside, but rather to lead us toward our potential and destiny. Of utmost importance is not what one gets out of a relationship, but what one brings to it. It is not only about the people who interact with each other, but the vehicle that shapes all life.

RELATIONSHIP MISTAKES CHECKLIST

Six mistakes to avoid in the beginning of any relationship:

1. Not asking enough questions
2. Ignoring warning signs of potential problems
3. Making premature compromises
4. Giving in to blind lust right away
5. Giving in to seduction
6. Putting commitment before compatibility

Couples who share similar values have more success in having a harmonious, lasting relationship. When there are opposite value systems present tension is created which causes bickering and fighting. When they are soul mates, all things are equal and easy. It is the same as if both people have been together previously. In soul mate encounters this is true, for both have been on this planet before as someone else and because they have a karmic debt to repay their path crosses in this lifetime and they "CONNECT", (actually they reconnect).

In choosing the right partner one must look for character, not simply looks or personality. A common thread is present where both have similar interests, ambition, and goals for the future.

15 QUALITIES TO LOOK FOR IN A SOUL MATE RELATIONSHIP

1. Commitment to learning, personal transformation
2. Emotionally open, compassionate
3. Integrity, honesty
4. Maturity, responsibility
5. Good self-esteem, self confident
6. Self-improvement
7. Positive attitude
8. Sharing ideas, opinions, and feelings
9. Trustworthiness
10. Sensitive
11. Passionate
12. Pride in self
13. Good self image
14. Cooperative
15. Sexual chemistry

FRIENDSHIP

"The glory of friendship is not in the outstretched hand, nor the kindly smile, nor the joy of companionship. It is the spiritual inspiration that comes to one when he discovers someone else believes and is willing to trust him."

Ralph Waldo Emerson

HOW TO RECOGNIZE YOUR SOUL MATE

The most satisfying relationship is when two people are romantically entwined. They radiate similar vibrations. The chance meeting of soul mates is predestined for their soul's growth. Ancient healers and mystics believed that each of us plays an important role in creating our own reality through the choices we make daily which help us to learn lessons involving love versus hate, power versus cooperation. It is through these kinds of lessons and challenges that the soul grows so that one can discover self. We know when we have found our counterparts because all learning is remembering the past. Humans are the sum total of all our experience from the beginning of time. During a lifetime an individual could come into contact with thousands of soul mates among his or her peers. How one works, plays, dreams, aspires, thinks, and relates to others - this is LIFE. Life is a reflection of all our previous lifetimes. All life experience is evaluated and taken into consideration in looking at each other's personality. Shared past lives is the prerequisite for a soul mate relationship in this lifetime.

> "Think not you can direct the course of love, for love, if it finds you worthy, directs your course."
>
> Kahil Gibran

SOUL MATES CONNECT ON THREE LEVELS

(1) Desire
(2) Intent
(3) True Love

The soul mate union teaches and supports both partners. The point is not knowing another person or learning to love another person. It is how we are able to welcome others into our hearts. "If you love someone, put their name in a circle instead of a heart, because hearts can break but circles go on forever."

The greatest connection one can have is with self, which determines the quality of all relationships throughout life with others. Love is attracted and all relationships continue to express love and joy. Every stage in life exists to serve us and to bring each of us closer to happiness and to love. Each stage teaches us how to trust our heart allowing more love into our lives.

"Love makes time pass. Time makes love pass."

Euripides

HOW CAN I FIND MY SOUL MATE?

The expression, "No risk, no gain" is true with respect to soul mates. One must reach out and enter into life's mainstream by becoming involved, enrolling in a class, volunteering or working within a group setting. This action shakes up the energy around the person bringing new individuals into their life. Socializing and trying new activities are a few ways to meet your soul mate. Experiencing new places or activities helps soul mates locate their own element.

"Your vision will become clear only when you look into your heart. Who looks outside, dreams. Who looks inside, awakens."

Carl Jung

THE FOUNDATION OF THE SOUL MATE SYMBOL

Friendship, Honor, Trust, Respect, Spontaneity,

Affection, Love

Just as any building or structure has a base, or floor that supports it, in a soul mate relationship, the foundation of this union consists of the above traits.

These elements are the basis of soul mate. Without them, the soul mate structure is not complete. These characteristics must be present during the courtship period, growing stronger as the relationship is cultivated and as it matures.

A discussion of the foundation follows:

FRIENDSHIP: In any relationship both people must first be friends. Friendships can be cultivated. This phase of a relationship can either grow and develop into "best friends" or remain simply friends, which would be in the same category as acquaintances.

HONOR: Each person in the relationship should honor the other. There should be no competition or one-upmanship between the two.

TRUST: Both individuals should be able to trust the other unconditionally.

RESPECT: Respect would be present in their eyes for one another. Neither would put the other down. A feeling of being proud of the other should be in the make-up.

SPONTANAITY: Spontaneous action is important. Spur of the moment ideas would come from the minds of the people involved.

EXAMPLES: "Let's go on a picnic!", "Want to go to the mountains for a look at the changing leaves right now?", "Maybe we should plan a future vacation", or "Do you want to start a saving account for vacation funds?"

AFFECTION: Affection is personal, a form of endearment between two people. It is best to keep personal touching private. Those who are openly affectionate in public are being overly demonstrative for the attention they can garner. True affection is felt without public displays.

LOVE: Love is the ultimate trait in the basic line-up of the floor of the soul mate symbol. It should take at least six months for anyone to declare their love for another. The first weeks of any relationship are exciting where lust plus infatuation are in the mix. Once the couple settles down in the coupling and go through the up and downs with one another and when six months have passed, love is the feeling that emerges.

> "It is not our purpose to become each other, it is to recognize each other, to learn and see the other and honor him for what he is."
>
> Hermann Hesse

Test for soul mates using palmistry: the baby finger from the opposite hand must be able to fit into the soul mate symbol on the palm. The baby finger must be laid on its side and slid into the area. If it fits in the area designated the possibility exists that soul mates from one's past lives can appear in this one.

SOUL MATE SYMBOL ON THE HUMAN PALM

Soul mate symbols can appear as a pyramid, an Indian Tee Pee or a pillow. They must be on the top 1/3 of the palm below the wrist.

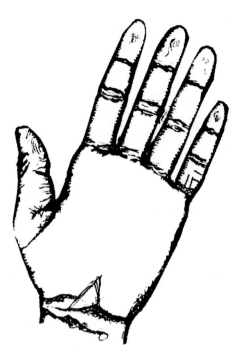

This symbol is located on the human palm by the wrist, looking toward the center of the hand.

There are five basic areas of a Soul Mate symbol.

Beginning at the bottom of the symbol and reading from bottom to top, they are as follows:

Communication

Visible Appearance of Couple

Spirituality

Sexual Compatibility

Similar Belief System

SOUL MATE SYMBOL MEANING:

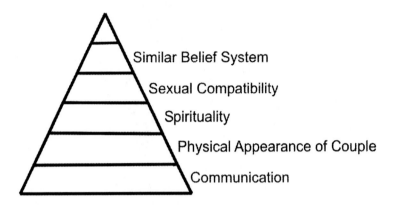

Similar Belief System

Sexual Compatibility

Spirituality

Physical Appearance of Couple

Communication

Note: The pyramid levels represent the variety of ways that two can connect on a deeper soul level with one another.

COULD I HAVE MORE THAN ONE SOUL MATE?

The answer is yes, if both you and the other person are old souls having lived in prior lifetimes. The marks found on the palm under the fingers and beneath the Life line denote a person's past lives. The average number of marks is between four and seven, each counting for one hundred years. If there are no marks at this location, the person is a new soul and cannot have a union with a soul mate. Markings on this spot could run into the hundreds, which would then show that those individuals did not work out their life lessons. They had to return to this world numerous times in order to accomplish and finish their karmic business with another.

Soul mates are worldly, awe-inspired, centered, grounded, in harmony with the earth, sensitive to each other's needs and able to focus. In a soul mate relationship life can be incredibly exciting and comfortable at the same time. There is a wonderful feeling of warmth and euphoria. Neither person criticizes or treats the other like a second-class citizen. They can talk; hold meaningful, lengthy conversations where each takes a turn speaking as the other listens.

> "People are like stained-glass windows. They sparkle and shine when the sun is out, but when darkness sets in, their true beauty is revealed only if there is a light from within."
>
> Elizabeth Kubler Ross

WHAT IS KARMA?

According to Oriental Palmistry, the definition of Karma: an action or deed, energy in action, the law of cause and effect, of retribution. It is seen as bringing upon oneself inevitable results, good or bad, either in this life or in reincarnation. It is unfinished business that was never resolved, or unlearned lessons from the past that need the combined attention of the soul mates. Karma encompasses all humanity and the universe.

It produces various forms of energy - some worthy, some which are harmful. Humans radiate with vibrations that give clues to one's personality and spirituality. In the realm of spirituality, soul mates acknowledge karma's existence. A "karmic relationship" describes friends, lovers or enemies who come together for the purpose of paying off their past life debts and for soul advancement.

Soul mates comprehend their spiritual connection, possessing knowledge from past lives. Both feel a magnetic pull. It is their personal connection to each other as they embark on a new beginning together. Souls never age, wrinkle, wear out or tire. No matter the number of years that may pass, each of us remains forever in this world, but in different housings as time marches on.

EXAMPLE: Two three-year-old boys living next door to each other until both reach old age: their friendship intact eighty years. They had a nasty fight

11

toward the end of their lives. In this lifetime they are two other people who carry that imprint from a past life. They meet in order to work out the details of why they were fighting bitterly in the previous lifetime. The relationship proceeds in this lifetime once they have completed their past issues. From one lifetime to the next, man determines his fate by his actions, thoughts, feelings, words and deeds.

Soul mates bring all the goodness they have learned and acquired from other lifetimes into this world, leaving earlier mistakes behind.

> Divine Love always has met and will always meet every human need.
>
> Mary Baker Eddy

IF YOU ARE MY SOUL MATE WHY ARE WE SO MISERABLE?

Soul work requires a widening of the heart and mind, trusting in and allowing fate to intervene. Soul mates can be both stimulating and demanding; they tend to bring out the best in each other. There are times in a union, however, when this is not true and one or both partners may ask themselves why they are so unhappy. Evidence suggests couples who argue and express themselves openly release stress and tension and their union lasts longer than those who "stuff their feelings" but who do not speak up. A great relationship consists of venting feelings when necessary to clear the air, then moving beyond that. They communicate easily.

At times soul mates miss the opportunity to connect with one another, as two ships passing in the night. One person may be hopelessly tied to another individual, unable to obtain his or her freedom when the other is available. This is sad because the reunion cannot take place. There is no reversal in some situations. Ideally, a soul mate arrives on the scene when his or her "other half " wishes to bond with someone who is a "match".

> "Destiny is not a matter of chance; it is a matter of choice. It is not a thing to be waited for; it is a thing to be achieved."
>
> William Jennings Bryan

WILL THIS SOUL MATE STAY FOR THE REST OF MY LIFE?

By asking the universe, the angels or one's higher self for guidance in meeting a partner he or she desires, it is possible for the miracle of soul mates to find one another. If a person is blocking, putting up walls, one must realize that this will prevent their soul mate from coming into their life. By preparing inner changes the path for a soul mate to enter is clear for perfect timing to occur. To attract a soul mate's attention, one's natural vibration must be turned up, like a lighthouse beacon in the night. A person with high energy can feel his or her soul mate's presence even if they are in a room filled with hundreds of people.

Having a soul mate in one's life increases awareness, alertness and constantly forces one to confront self. Like mirrors seeing each other's weaknesses and strengths, the couple can and do work on their problem areas to correct faults within each other. Soul mates give each other self-confidence. Together they have the power to make dramatic changes.

> At the innermost core of all loneliness is a deep and powerful yearning for union with one's lost self.
>
> Brendan Francis

WHAT DO SOUL MATES NEED?

1. HONESTY: Soul mates share their deepest secrets with each other. Instead of reacting, they explore and are curious and supportive.

2. GENEROSITY: Soul mates harbor no ulterior motives, expecting nothing in return. They give time energy, insight, empathy and compassion. They listen to one another and communicate openly and honestly.

3. EMPATHY: Soul mates feel for each other, without verbalizing, "You aren't alone, I'm here for you. I am feeling what you are going through."

4. FORGIVENESS: Soul mates grant pardons without resentment, they don't punish.

5. GRATITUDE: Soul mates appreciate life is a miracle, a gift, thankful for their partner.

6. SKILLS: Soul mates require effective communication, listening, resolving, problem solving, negotiating and compromising.

> "A true friend is someone who is there for you when they'd rather be anywhere else."
>
> Len Wein

REACTION OF SOUL MATES WITH EACH OTHER:

Conversation between soul mates is laid back. During the dating period there is no tension, friction, sexual frustration, competition or bickering. Soul mates think alike, reading one another's mind, fine-tuning in to each other's energy level harmoniously. Those who experience love feel good about them, respect and accept one another, sense when one requires a period of quiet time alone, or when a hug is needed. In times of stress, soul mates are 100% supportive. Since the partners are best friends, they may drop all their anxieties on each other.

14

Understanding one another's needs unconditionally, the union works in good as well as bad times. Soul mates are worldly, awe-inspired, centered and grounded in harmony with nature. Sensitive to each other's wishes, they are able to focus and converse freely. Soul mates are sounding boards for exchanging thoughts and guidance. They search for the answers to life's dilemmas together.

> "It's not what is happening to you in this lifetime, but what has happened to you in the past that determines who you will become in the future. It is your decision about what to focus on, what things mean to you and what you're going to do about those issues that set your ultimate destiny."
>
> Anthony Robbins

WHEN IS MY SOUL MATE ARRIVING?

In order for a soul mate to enter anyone's life, he or she must first establish a friendship, then they become best friends, and in doing so they learn if they are truly soul mates. Friendship is an attraction and the magnetism of souls, not a union of personalities. Intimate friends are soul mates. Sometimes friendships bloom in an instant; at other times they must be cultivated.

Loyalty and feelings can sustain friendships that are a blending of intimacy and individuality. In the development of all kinds of friendships the communication must be open to allow a soul mate's entry. Individuals must participate in new activities to draw new energy to them in order to expand the horizon.

Every living thing – plants, animals and humans have a soul. The memory of past lives is carried forward in the cell structure. Humans have numerous connections to others during each lifetime. These can be mental, emotional, physical and sexual connections that people experience when they are involved.

EXAMPLES:

A man and woman of similar age may be soul mates, but they could also be family. Two men may hit it off famously, alike in mentality. There is no sexual connection between them, only a bonding of friendship. Two women may be able to open up to each other; the realization they are soul sisters from a time long ago allows them to continue their friendship in this lifetime.

"Life is about knowing, having to change, taking the moment and making the best of it without knowing what's going to happen next."

Gilda Radner

WILL I CONNECT WITH MY SOUL MATE?

To connect with your soul mate you must open your soul to your deepest feelings, hurts and desires. It is that part of our psyche that we most vigorously defend. We must drop our defenses. Often, we hide these parts of ourselves because of ego. To open our soul, we must stop protecting it. Because we speak the truth from the depths of who we are we must trust and believe in self, know our hearts desire and go after it. This requires strength and an inner courage. The universe sends to each of us that which we most deeply need if we are free to accept it. We must be willing to risk the sacrifice of ego for the potential reward of a fulfilling relationship with someone who really knows and loves us with no strings attached - our soul mate.

LIFE'S MESSAGE

A gigantic message board of life reads: "BE YOURSELF" - for truthfulness is the strongest aphrodisiac, the only real way to keep the romance flowing in a close love relationship.

Truth produces a greater aliveness between two people more so than anything else in the world. Soul power is a creative, loving reality simply waiting to awaken within the consciousness of each person.

THE DEFINITION OF LOVE:

Love is an action that is within our power involving various behaviors and skills throughout life. We cultivate the vibration that exists within each of us. This is a bond that connects us to our greatest resources. When you're beloved, rather than ego becomes the center of your concern, then you are in love. Love and the human spirit are our most enduring gifts from God. The purpose of life is "growth". Soul mates are relationships of growth. We grow to love and love to grow, thus we merge with the Universal Intelligence, (God).

Numerous relationships develop from the soul's desire to experience "growth". The light of love is passed from heart to heart; a connection with all creation. The deepest need of the soul is to find and to receive love. True love in daily living is enduring and mutually satisfying to both partners. It is giving unselfishly and it is receiving. True love allows life to flow spontaneously. We should not control it or insist on structuring it in a rigid format.

Love is a stepping-stone in the development of an individual. It is the total commitment to another person. We can visualize and manifest a soul mate. The joy of life is taking raw material we each possess and making sparkling gems and intricate, colorful tapestries out of it. Soul mates produce powerful energy together. They are a force of their own. A new energy, one that is fresh and boundless in its own identity is formed out of the union. Vibrations of love teach soul mates to grow. Change occurs gradually. We must learn to trust our hearts for the point is not in knowing another person, but in discovering how tender we can bear to be with them. What good manners can we show as we welcome others into our heart?

> "Love means setting aside walls and fences, unlocking doors and saying YES. . . one can enter paradise simply by saying YES to the moment."
>
> Pat Rodegast

WHAT IS A TWIN FLAME?

The definition of a twin flame: a mirror image of self; there are no barriers between them. Soul mate couples who are twin flames are usually similar in appearance, belief systems and likes, dislikes and abilities, sharing much in common. There are no rules set down in love because they are one in spirit and in their spiritual origin. Twin flames are partners in the truest sense, similar in outlook and they are compatible. Their soul development is at the same level and they work well together, are project-oriented, well-mated, often with similar facial features and physiques. They're inner ties run deep, beyond just companionship. They possess a combination of mind, spirit and soul with the secret longings and aspirations of their love partners. They are both in tune to the God mind, Universal Intelligence.

Relationships that touch the soul connect us into a dialogue with eternity and Divinity itself. Relationships may experience difficulties in the beginning where emotions may be strong but confusing. Many share the experience of drama and ecstasy, of discovering and possibly losing their soul mates, not just in this lifetime but in other lifetimes as well. A true twin soul mate is the other half of self.

> "Life without love is like a tree without blossoms or fruit."
>
> Kahlil Gilbran

SEX IS IN EXISTENCE ON EVERY LEVEL OF HUMAN RELATIONSHIP

Sex is a profound, far-reaching aspect of the soul, bringing together body, mind, emotion and imagination in an intense mental and physical experience that touches every fiber of one's being. Sex offers guidance where strong emotions reside. This is a form of education, not just the expression of love, but rather an aspect of one's entire life. Issues worrying someone can affect the intensity of lovemaking for better or worse. The soul is affected more by our treatment of desire and longing than by one's failure to get things right.

Likes attract, opposites oppose; compatibility is that which holds all kinds of relationships together. Carl Jung discussed the magical way life sets the stage for the soul to reside in motion. It is our invitation to adventure, a phenomenon that lures one away from normal routines. Life itself can be a playful mood. Sex can be an inquiry of the inner child to reach the depths of soul, to show oneself, to come out and play. Casting away doubts, the fear of being hurt and able to give and receive love are desired by all of us. Soul mates have, in the past, separated and lived apart so they can appreciate each other that much more when they reunite. The value of having a soul mate in one's life increases one's understanding and capacity to love. An external reality, a soul mate is a dual inner reality that may not be realized by one or both partners unless interacting love exists.

MY
DIARY OF
PALM READING
SESSIONS

Love, Romance and Soul
Mate Relationships
1957 to 2001

#1 I READ ERMA BOMBECK'S HAND: May 1956

While working at a newspaper in Dayton Ohio I met a young columnist who drove in weekly from Miamisburg, an adjoining town. She arrived at the office with her written columns, and then lounged around the editorial department waiting for her galleys. My assignment was typesetting her material on the hot metal linotype equipment. She proofread her own columns (three a week). We quickly formed a warm friendship and traded smart quips back and forth. She was aware I was a part time high school student and confided she was a few years older than I. Her name was Erma Bombeck.

I had transferred to the Classified Department when Erma approached me one spring day. She whispered, "I've heard the juicy gossip around the newspaper plant you read palms. Will you read me?"

"I'd love to read your hand, Erma," I answered. "I'll sign out and we'll find a quiet place with good light."

We sat on a sunny stairwell with intense light from a high ceiling window. I distinctly remember Erma offered me both hands.

"Which palm do you read?" she inquired. "I use both of my hands."

I replied, "After I study both of your palms, I'll know which one I want."

"You go girlfriend. Do whatever you have to do," she laughed.

I peered closely at both palms and discovered she was truly a left and right-handed individual, her brain developed evenly on both sides.

"Your Life line isn't too long," I began. "It details life into your seventies where you'll cram a lifetime into the years you are here," I predicted.

"What else do you see?" she asked, interested.

"Your Love line is a perfect textbook example, showing one marriage, at age twenty, to a man a few years your senior. It's a solid, unbroken line denoting a heavy duty connection, the man of your dreams," I explained. "You possess many talents and untapped potential, abilities yet to be discovered. You could have been a teacher, a trainer, or a tour guide because you have a knack of expressing yourself, a dramatic flair that makes people pay attention to you. They comprehend your message."

"Good news! I love writing; it is my way of expressing. I take an every day situation and poke fun at it. I always look for humor in everything I come in contact with and make fun of myself too," she admitted.

I stated, "Work is important to you. Because of your two small children it's better for you to work from home. You get to mother them and write too, allowing you the best of both worlds. Your creativity hasn't hit full tilt yet. You are just at the tip of the iceberg."

"You are so full of it!" she laughed, "I would love it though if you were right about my career. When I sat down you mentioned my brain was developed on both sides. I don't understand the concept."

I defined, "If you were only able to function with your right hand the left side of your brain would be active as the logical, methodical, practical one. The right brain would be the creative one, the dreamer. If you were only left-handed it would be the opposite. In your case both sides of the brain are equally active all the time."

"So I'm a unique human being?" she joked.

"You are what you make of yourself. I believe you're poised, competent, self-confident, an individual who loves life and lives it to the fullest," I said.

"I'm pretty happy with my life," she exclaimed. "Have you heard? My column is being picked up by the Cox newspaper organization, going into syndication. Am I excited! It means more money, more interviews and more exposure. I'll be standing tall!"

We discussed her children, a boy and girl. She wondered if they would have any siblings. I noted four marks on her baby finger, indicating four possible pregnancies.

"I hope your prediction comes true, we do want four kids," she giggled. "I wonder, should I write a book? I planned to do stories about the suburbs, my home life, similar to my column. Would worldly people be interested in reading my autobiography?" she asked seriously.

"Your Work line is lit up like a Christmas tree telling me you're really in tune to writing a book. The idea is appealing and I feel you will do it. After your first book you will continue writing," I counseled.

"When do you see me gaining popularity with the public? I'm twenty-seven," she uttered under her breath.

"You're on the cusp of fame now. I see a period spanning forty-five years of a successful writing career," I offered.

"I can't thank you enough for this stimulating and enlightening palm reading Myrna! I'm going home to think about the book writing idea," she gushed.

We hugged each other warmly and parted company.

#2   I BEGGED HIM, "PLEASE DON'T LEAVE": September 1957

I was a freshman in college when I became acquainted with a young woman who lived in my neighborhood. We carpooled with several students to Ohio University in Athens Ohio. Early one morning at her house, waiting for our ride she requested a palm reading. She told me she was in love with a man who was no longer in her life.

We discussed how he bowed out of the relationship after two steady years. Calmly, she described the wonderful times that they shared, then the dam broke. First came a flood of tears, then wailing and chest pounding in obvious pain.

"I inquired, "Should I leave the room? Do you want to be alone?"

She shook her head and through the tears I read the relief in her eyes.

"I haven't mentioned our breaking up to a anyone since last July," she sniffed. "I've never heard a word from him in all that time."

I suggested they needed time apart because he missed his friends, working out in the gym, and attending ball games. She said he told her his routines had been stifled since the beginning of their relationship. He produced a schedule that contained no time for them to spend together. It was a heartless, callus way of ending their relationship, the path he used to walk out of her life. He brought a finality to their romance with the prepared schedule.

"Why do you think he ended it?" I questioned.

"He said we were getting "too serious" at our age, that his grades slipped, and he lost touch with his buddies. He never went to the gym or to tryouts for athletics. Like that was my fault! I gave up my girlfriends and activities too. I just wanted to spend all my time with him. He meant more to me than anything or anybody else!" she sniffed.

I asked, "Did you step graciously aside and give him his freedom?"

"Of course not! I sobbed, the typical clinging vine. I begged him to stay with me. He's my soul mate; I just know it in my heart! I have issues with desertion. It hurt like a knife wound when he packed his personal belongings and walked away from me," she whimpered.

We talked about school, grades, anything except the lost love issue. I told her there were plenty of nice guys available. There was no response. Our ride honked and we scrambled to collect our belongings and stowed them in the trunk of the car.

The woman lived in my dormitory, on the main floor, one section down from mine. We ran into each other daily, either in the cafeteria or at the dorm mailboxes. We greeted each other politely, but never stood around talking. One day I noticed that she looked thin and pale. Her hair wasn't combed and she walked woodenly.

"Want to double date with me on Friday night? We're going swimming at the indoor pool across the street," I asked brightly.

She surprised me, smiled and agreed to go. The men called for us at 8:00 P.M. as prearranged. I introduced her and we walked to the campus pool. I swam and ducked the boys, laughing; having fun for quite awhile when I noticed my girlfriend was hanging on to the edge of the pool. She motioned for me to swim over to her.

" I can't stand being with another guy," she sighed. "This evening reminds me too much of HIM. I feel really terrible and I'm ruining the evening for my date too. I think I'll go back to the dorm."

Shocked by her antisocial behavior, I quietly explained we were two couples, out for the evening and if she were to ditch her date I would be left with two men. "You owe this night to yourself. You should stay, " I pleaded selfishly. "You'll loosen up and enjoy yourself if you just give this guy a chance. He's nice and he likes you too. It won't kill you to hang out . . . after all curfew is midnight, only a few hours away."

She didn't answer, but remained glued to the edge of the pool. She never uttered a single word after our discussion. When the closing bell sounded we left the water.

I told the boys we'd meet them in the lobby in twenty minutes. We showered, dressed, dried our hair and put on make-up. I tried unsuccessfully to engage my friend in a friendly conversation. She turned from me silently and looked at the floor.

At midnight we said good night to our dates and entered the dorm. Still she didn't speak. I was tired so I left her at the door to her section and went into my own. I thought that she was moody and would get over it.

At 4:00 A.M. I awoke with a start. She was standing next to my bunk, staring at me, looking frail, lonely and frightened.

"What's wrong?" I whispered quietly, being considerate of my roommate sleeping on the top bunk.

"Do you have any pills?" she inquired. "I need lots of pills. I want meds NOW!"

I told her I had no medications on hand.

"Your Mom's a nurse and I know she fixed up a medicine chest for you to keep at school. I could raid it," she responded.

I shook myself awake, stunned to see she was serious.

She blurted out, "I don't want to live anymore!"

"I think you ought to go to bed," I said soothingly. "We'll talk in the morning."

At 7:00 A.M. a student from her floor section entered their communal bathroom to take a shower. She screamed as she walked into a gruesome scene; my friend had hung herself in the shower stall.

#3 "THE MONSTER": October 1958

I was a part time radio announcer at WOUB, a 50,000-watt campus radio station in Athens Ohio, while attending college. The engineer paired with me for three weekly shows during those two years was declared legally blind. We got along famously as I was able to read his moods, his emotional state and his energy level prior to every program we worked on together.

One day a group of students lounged with coffee in the Speech Building Lobby. "E" asked me to read his palm. I asked if he wanted it read privately or in front of the gang clustered around the table. He replied we were his friends and I could read him there. I studied his lines and his session began.

"You were a precocious child, into everything," I affirmed. "Does that sound like you?"

"Yes, I was sighted then, with lots of activities. I played with neighborhood kids who called me "monster". I've always had an inquisitive mind and it drove everybody crazy," he admitted.

"Were you involved in a terrible car accident in your teens with a family member?" I inquired.

"Yes, my Dad. I was in eighth grade when IT happened. It was an awful scene, what I remember anyway," he offered.

"I see you trapped inside the vehicle for several hours until the Fire Department used the Jaws of Life to extricate you from the tangled auto. As they were lifting you out of the mangled car a terrific wind blew out of nowhere causing the car door to slam into your head," I explained.

"That's what they say happened," he replied, sadly.

"You weren't expected to live after such a blow to the head," I stated matter-of-factly.

He said he was in the hospital in a coma for many weeks. We discussed his survival mode; he was a fighter. He admitted his constitution and mental make-up were probably the reasons he lived through the trauma. Everyone sitting at the table listened intently to our conversation. The tension was evident.

"When I came out of the coma I was blind". I cried. "I asked everyone why me? I hated everybody! I hated being blind for a long time, then one day I decided if God allowed me to live He wanted me to go on with my life, not feel sorry about what happened to me," he explained.

"You enrolled in a school for the blind where you excelled at everything taught there and adjusted to your condition. I see you achieved straight A's for grades. Did you win a scholarship to college?" I questioned.

"You know my deepest secret. How's my life today?" he asked quietly.

"I see you are happy, with many friends, you earn good grades and manage many extra curricular activities along with a part time job at the radio station," I reported.

"So far you have me pegged. What about girls in my blind life? he inquired. "I want my soul mate, that special girl."

"Give it time. I'm a romantic and believe there is someone for each of us. One day you'll find the love you seek and you will marry," I predicted.

He asked about career opportunities, saying he understood many companies wouldn't consider him because of his handicap. He wondered if he would be able to earn a living after graduation to support a family some day. I saw his future was bright and told him so.

He thanked me sincerely for his palm reading session. The group around the table sat quietly, thinking. After a few minutes of silence, en masse, we returned to the radio station to work on details for the next day's programming.

#4 B'NAI BRITH: November 1960

Newly married in 1960, I joined a local chapter of B'nai Brith, a Jewish women's group. I accepted the responsibilities of Program Co-Chair. My partner was a married woman with twenty-year old twins. Meeting at someone's home to plan a Donor Luncheon for the following month, we outlined the entertainment for the event. Two weeks later she dropped a bombshell.

"My husband and I are going on vacation for two weeks. Everything's under control for the luncheon, all you'll be responsible for is taking the reservations. We're due home the day before and we can get together to discuss things then," she said.

"How can you leave now?" I whined. "I've never even been to a Donor Luncheon, let alone been a Co-Chair."

"Don't be such a baby! Just handle it will you darling?" she coaxed. "By the way, before we take off will you read my palm?"

We met at her house. I noticed her Life line was short but said nothing. "Your health is great; you only went through childbirth once. You could have produced two additional children. I see you were a fertile young woman, but after the twins, you chose not to have any more children."

"You sure are right about that," she laughed.

"Let me see your Love line?" I asked. "I believe you married your soul mate straight out of college. He was a late bloomer, eight or ten years older than you. You had many romantic experiences before you met him. It shows you married at age twenty-two."

31

"I can't believe you saw that by reading my hand," she said amazed.

We left together, arm in arm. She insisted on taking me to lunch after her palm reading session to pay me back. She was pleased. "You were so accurate and entertaining too. You should conduct a lecture on palmistry at the Donor Luncheon and be our guest speaker. We should lose the artist we hired," she exclaimed.

After lunch, as we walked to our respective cars she yelled, "You're a trooper, I know you can carry on if anything happens."

Two weeks later on the morning of the Donor Luncheon I received a tearful phone call from one of her twin daughters. "Mom and Dad were driving home from Florida in a rainstorm in Georgia when they were involved in a head-on collision, killed instantly."

#5   I'M WRITING A BOOK: January 1964

I worked for a weekly newspaper, the Times Review, on the night shift, as a typesetter in Dayton Ohio. An older, distinguished looking black gentleman worked there a few nights each week. He used a typesetting machine next to mine.

"I'm writing a book," he announced one night. I peered over his shoulder to see what he was writing. We became friendly, exchanging polite hellos, jokes and sometimes we shared food on breaks. One night around midnight he asked me to read his palm.

I studied his hand. "Your Life line has me worried. There are some medical conditions you're going to encounter in your fiftieth year. You are in your early forties now aren't you?" I inquired.

"Not real good at guessing ages are you?" he laughed. "I'm forty-nine this September. What do you see about my health?"

I explained he was burning the candle at both ends, pushing himself too hard. I asked him about relaxation. He said there was no time for it. I realized he enjoyed creative writing but clearly saw it was exhausting. "You are your own best friend and own worst enemy," I predicted.

"I plan to slow the pace once the book is finished, but right now I have deadlines - the pressure is on. I'm the Reverend at Church; I put in a good 40 hours plus every week, counting services, counseling sessions, you can imagine how it is in the life. This project is my joy, my baby and I love it," he explained.

"Your Love line shows you are a one-woman person. You met in college, and after your graduation, married. You are soul mates and both of you knew right away. You were 22 or 23," I offered.

He replied, "Right! We had two biggies that June, graduation and our wedding ceremony."

"You could have fathered four children. How many did you have?" I questioned.

He answered, "Four! You seem to be hitting me perfectly young lady," he laughed. "We produced four outstanding, beautiful sons."

Changing the subject, I asked him, "What's your book about?"

"The title is *The Spokes of the Wheel*. It explains grasping opportunities to get ahead in the business world. It outlines setting goals to achieve the desired result. The hints given here are applicable for any type of business. I discovered there aren't any comparable books like mine on the market. It's unique! I'm writing it in-between ministering," he explained.

"Good luck with it. Everybody could benefit from it," I replied. "It sounds interesting and I know you express yourself easily. If it's conversational and easily understood, you'll do well with it."

A few months passed; I noticed his absence and inquired at the front desk. I learned he had a massive heart attack. I sent him a funny, cheerful get well card. One evening about a month later he strolled through the newspaper office and stopped at my station.

"I'm not working, just visiting," he assured me. "Thanks for the jazzy get-well card. My publisher sent a copy of my book while I was hospitalized. You warned me to slow down but I refused to listen. Here's my autographed book in case I become famous someday," he joked.

It was signed, "To the palm reader who predicted my book would be a success once completed, but health problems would be in my future."

#6   THIS BLACKMAIL IS KILLING ME: September 1971

While newly employed in Indianapolis at a publication company I encountered many interesting people. Word spread in the company that I was a palmist. I was constantly approached for readings and conducted them before and after work, on lunch hours and on break. A couple in my department asked for a double reading.

An Editor, "S", a dark-haired twenty-eight year old woman, sat in a cubicle nearby. "K" was a fifty-year-old Senior Editor. His office was directly across the hall from hers in the executive area. They had been dating secretly for six months before the news of their romantic fling circulated among the office gossips. She was single; he was married twenty-one years, the father of four.

I read "S" first, in the Audio Room explaining her Life line denoted a strong, healthy family background. I saw no major illnesses in her future. I told "S" there were no whimpy people in her lineage and that longevity was unmistakable. She didn't want to hear a discussion on life minutiae, but instead pleaded with me to look at her Love line. I informed her the expectation of "K" 's leaving his family to marry her was unrealistic. I saw they were deeply in love, connected on mental, religious, emotional, and spiritual levels, compatible sexually. I detected their physical attraction played a large part in the relationship. I realized they were communicating well. "S" had the soul mate symbol on her hand so I explained my definition of a soul mate using Oriental Palmistry.

Ecstatic, she cried, "Yes! We are connected in all ways, and we look great together. We have many commonalties too."

"Trust and honesty must be in the scenario too," I counseled.

Nodding her head she exclaimed, "We have it!"

I began calmly, "You trust him, but what about his wife and children? He cheats on them to spend time with you. He hasn't been totally honest."

She admitted he was deceitful in order to create their time together. Her session finished, she thanked me and left.

"K" stepped in. Holding his outstretched palm in mine I intuitively picked up something sinister happening in his life. "What's going on these days?" I asked. "K" stiffened. I was shocked to feel such intensity and the energy shift so quickly. "Do you want to share information with me?" I questioned.

Shaking, tearfully he explained he and "S" started as co-workers, were friends, and then got involved. He described his wife, his beautiful children, their lovely home and his career responsibilities at the company. He sat quietly for a minute, and then plunged into a discussion of the hell he and "S" were living in. He informed me of a note retrieved from his desk a month earlier, threatening to notify his wife of their indiscretion if he didn't pay the "hush money" to keep their silence. Scared, silently he complied and paid their demand. Per instructions, "K" left an envelope taped to the back of a designated candy vending machine in the Break Room. Two weeks later a second note mysteriously appeared on his desk. The note-writer demanded additional money. The first request was $25.00 in small bills. The second stated five $10.00 bills should be left on the vending machine back with a weekly payment from then on.

"K" and "S" discussed their dilemma and wondered how they could continue paying if the amount escalated. On the fifth week a nastier, hand-written memo appeared on "K" ' s desk with a $100.00 demand. It was then, he said he marched into his Supervisor's office, produced the note and explained their predicament. Behind closed doors they discussed his romantic entanglement. His boss was displeased to learn his Senior Editor and Editor were having an affair, but the blackmail scheme someone in the company was orchestrating enraged him. He suggested "K" call the police immediately.

Scared to death, "K" announced, "The last note threatened if $100.00 wasn't on the vending machine by 4:00 PM that day harm would come to "S".

I offered, "If this was my problem I'd call the police today. I would beg my family to understand my indiscretions even though I didn't deserve their mercy."

"What's to become of "S" and I?" "K" inquired.

"That's up to the two of you. Once this blackmail scheme is finished you'll be free to do whatever you both want," I responded.

He thanked me for the creative input in his reading and left the Audio Room, the burden of it hanging heavy on his shoulders. "S" and "K" huddled in her enclosure in a serious debate as I passed by. Several hours later they approached my desk and announced several mutual decisions. They were going to call the police, talk to his family and after the extortionist was caught, planned to resign. "K" said he was going to file for divorce, looking at a future move to Florida. They decided to start their lives over. I was delighted my palmistry skills had assisted them in finding the path that would eventually end their torment.

#7   THE WIDOW: March 1972

While working as an administrative assistant at an ITT subsidiary in Indianapolis I met a woman whose office was across the hall from mine. She was beautiful, a young mother and newly widowed. Early one morning before anyone arrived, she whispered to me as she walked by my desk, "Would you read my hand?"

We chose the lunchroom on the eleventh floor at one o'clock.

"I'm anxious to see what you discover about my life," she confided. "I've never done this."

At the designated time we met and I studied her palm. We talked about her Life line and discussed her health. I mentioned she was careful and protective with her children. I noticed her eyes growing sad. She tensed, became agitated. She was very interested in having a reading, but for a moment slipped to a far off place. I brought her back to reality.

"An accident your husband encountered left you a widow. You begged him to give up whatever it was he participated in but he refused. Understanding his life dream, with dread in your heart, every day when he left you feared harm would come to him. His work, a lifetime hobby that became his livelihood, was his most precious love," I reported.

37

Thoughtfully she related, "Yes my darling's life was his work. He was in an auto accident, killed instantly in a collision during a practice session in a race car at the Indy 500."

"I'm so sorry," I sympathized. "I didn't know the details, only what I picked up from you".

"I'm questioning life and the kids," she sighed. "Will they be OK? My fifteen-year-old son is full of so much anger! He's mad at me for not insisting I stop his father's racing. My daughter's thirteen and needs a male influence in her life. I'm both mother and father and it's not easy."

"There will be future problems with your children," I predicted. "I can't candy-coat it for you. They need counseling. I envision you dating in the future. You will find a man who will love and nurture you. You'll rediscover love and he will lift your spirits and pull you out of this depression. Your kids won't accept him at first. They'll try to drive you apart; they won't succeed because he is strong, a man who is giving, caring, loving, sensitive, a wonderful human being. Given what you've been through this person will be a God-send."

She digested what I said, calmed down and stopped fidgeting.

"Was your daughter Daddy's little girl?" I asked her in a soothing voice.

She answered, "Yes, he idolized her since the day she was born. He loved our son too, of course, but in a different way."

I said, "Did this accident happen about a year and a half ago?"

"Exactly fifteen months ago," she replied, "I . . . this has been the most distasteful period in my entire life. I go to work, home, cry, climb into my empty bed and talk to my husband every night. I hate my life! At times I hate my kids too! Why did God allow this to happen to our family?" she questioned through tears. Blowing her nose she continued, "Some days I just wish I didn't have to face my kids. It seems to get worse everyday. I explained race car drivers are a different breed. They get racing in their system and that's it. They just don't get it," she said, sighing.

"Do you do anything for recreation? Are you involved in anything at Church or at school?" I questioned.

She responded, "I go out, but it hurts like hell. I attend school functions and meetings but every kid there has two parents. I go to the Rec but I can't force myself to stay. Nothing appeals to me."

I offered, "I think you need a vacation from self. The issues you have with God, your children, even the racing industries are weighing heavily on your shoulders. Let up a little. If someone invites you out, even for lunch, simply allow yourself to participate."

"I couldn't stand anyone near me, or even being kind, pulling out a chair for me in a restaurant. That would give me stomach pains. I know I can't handle it," she cried.

"Have you gone into counseling in the last fifteen months?" I inquired. "Are their support groups, maybe a widow-widowers group or some club you could join?"

"I have gone to meetings. I sit alone and end up going home early. I cry on the way home and after I get there too. So what's the use?" she sobbed.

"It appears you married your high school sweetheart," I stated. "I believe he was the only man in your life, ever. You were soul mates. You never dated anyone else, never tasted life, except from his cup. You have no previous experience to call upon. That's the reason the transition from marriage to widowhood is so troubling."

"You are right! I have never bedded another man and I can't imagine myself with anyone else, ever," she sighed. "I'm so lonely! I feel empty, like a shell of a person."

We sat quietly until she calmed down. I suggested she find a therapy that would enable her to move past the stuck place. I explained a period of grieving was necessary, but prolonging it indefinitely was a sure way to make her ill.

"Find a way to gain control of your roller coaster emotions," I suggested. "Fifteen months is long enough to suffer. You have to get on with your life."

She agreed to seek professional help and thanked me for her session.

#8   I'M ALL ALONE AND I DON'T LIKE IT: October 1973

While living in Florida I greeted an older gentleman every day walking my beagle, Tammy. He would sit on his front porch until he spied us approaching, and then walk to the sidewalk in front of his house to greet us. Being polite, I always conversed with him for a few minutes, sensing his loneliness. Instinctively I knew he needed human companionship. I wanted to continue walking to the beach, but it seemed such a tiny good deed, that for a few minutes each day I gave him my full attention.

"I'm all alone in this enormous house and I dislike it," he admitted.

One day he invited me to sit on his porch for a visit. He had a magnificent view of the Inner Coastal Waterway, so I agreed.

"I notice you enjoy watching the boats, he said, "I wanted you to see the view from my vantage point. Come sit down on my porch and I'll make some iced tea."

Tammy and I waited on the well-furnished porch, our special walking time slipping away. Finally, he returned with the tea. Tammy napped at my feet.

"I have a request," he began, "Can you read my palm? I'd be happy to pay you for your time."

Anxious, I would have done anything to hurry the visit along so I agreed. "Where are you from?" I asked.

He replied, "New Jersey."

"From studying your Work line I can see where you ran a family business for many years under a great deal of pressure," I offered.

"I got pressure from my wife, family, friends, the police, and my customers. It was never ending, but I handled it," he remarked.

"What did you do?" I questioned.

"You won't believe this! I was the sole operator of a Porno shop for twenty-nine years that was completely controlled by the Mob," he replied in a matter-of-fact tone. "I got relieved of duty."

Changing the subject, I stated "You suffered a terrible loss in your family last year."

"Yes, I lost my soul mate, my beloved wife, Mama; she had a heart attack. The strain finally got her, with the police constantly calling or stopping at the house for me. I was involved in illegal deals every day. I miss Mama real bad," he admitted, eyes misty.

"This home you are living in was purchased by your children. Am I right? They wanted you to retire from the Mob. They love you and this was their way of insuring your safety. They couldn't face losing you too," I reported.

"Yeah, they love their old man. They show up down here for vacations once in awhile. I stay here alone. My life's no picnic, let me tell you," he responded, sadly.

"So you retired early, were you ready to give it up?" I inquired.

"I wasn't retirement age and I wasn't ready for the farm either but the kids forced the issue and made me quit. They said Mama would be alive today if I wasn't connected to the Mob. At the store I saw so many dysfunctional sexual deviates it felt normal after awhile. I was a friend with the transvestites, prostitutes, the peek-a-boo dirty movie watchers, the nuts, the drug dealers, and all the rest. The store was a front for Mob meetings. I looked the other way when they needed a meeting place," he explained.

Fascinated by his dialogue I forgot about the dog's walk. "Were you sorry to leave it behind?" I inquired.

"I didn't yell much when they took my shop. I thought I was being demoted and they were taking control," he explained.

"What did you do for them?" I asked, interested.

"I was the front man. They raked in tons of money; I kept their books and got paid handsomely for that chore. There were two sets of financial books, you see, their set, which was the real one, and the one for the IRS. I massaged that set of books. I made it look good. I oversaw a lot of young employees too," he offered. "I know a lot about their dirty business! The Mob said my mind snapped after we lost Mama so they let me out of their contract, no muss, no fuss. It usually doesn't go down smooth like that, if you grasp my meaning. Either you're Company for life, or you got none," he said, his throat catching.

"Look at it this way, now you're a man of leisure, living in the Florida sun," I laughed. "Why don't you forget the past and enjoy your new life. You could meet people from the East Coast here, many in your age group. You could fill your hours with all kinds of activities and friendships. You have a lot in common with some of the senior citizens here."

He answered, "I know, I know."

I stood up to leave and told him I would stop by the following day with Tammy to say hello.

He hugged me tightly and thanked me for his reading. I thanked him for his hospitality and headed down the sidewalk toward the ocean.

As I reached the public sidewalk he leaned over the front railing and in a whisper said, "I value your friendship, and I'm grateful for your time with me. Thanks for being here."

#9 I'M TIRED OF TRAINING HUSBANDS: July 1974

I taught Drama and Arts and Crafts at a Day Camp in West Hialeah Florida. The Director requested a palm reading as we sat under a tree at morning ceremonies. She was trying to reach a decision on whether or not to permit me to teach palmistry to the children in my drama class. I looked at her palm. It was swollen because she was in her eighth month of pregnancy. I saw a history of two failed marriages. This one was her third time in marriage. She was a tall, blonde woman, stubborn, set in her ways.

"I hope this relationship is my last," she sighed. "I'm forty years old and I'm getting tired of training husbands. At least this time I picked a care-giver, not a taker."

"I wonder, what's different in this relationship?" I inquired.

"I found a man compatible with me. We are soul mates. We get along famously. He's a 100% support system for me and I give him the same. We are alike, where husbands #1 and #2 were both the opposite of me," she said.

"You're at the same place in your lives," I explained. "That's why this union works so well."

We discussed the arrival of their new baby. She was already a mother to three other children from previous marriages.

"What about work?" she asked. "Will I put in these long hours for the rest of my adult life?"

"You'll miss a few weeks of work after the baby is born, then return to your position," I reported.

"Oh great! Just what I didn't want to hear," she laughed.

I described her as hard working, detail-oriented, a promoter, and an organizer, meticulous on paperwork. She was a softie with problem children, always trying to help them, a fun Day Camp Director. We discussed her work ethic, teaching ability, and management techniques. She said she possessed a lot of natural intuition.

"Do you see a family vacation in the near future?" she asked.

"No travel for the next year for your family," I replied.

"Darn, I wanted to get away from south Florida after the baby. It's so darn hot," she exclaimed. "You have your craft down to a science," she exclaimed. "You are specific in the explanation of the lines on the palm. I have come to the conclusion you can teach the kids Oriental Palmistry today. Learning this skill will enrich their lives. I can see them going home from Camp telling their parents they were taught palmistry today. They will be able to read their families once they master it."

I thanked her for the opportunity to teach Palmistry at the Day Camp.

#10 TWO KIDS WATCHING OVER HER: June 1978

For seven years in Indianapolis my next door neighbors were a charming, older couple. He had cancer and died during surgery. A few months later the newly widowed neighbor saw me in the backyard gardening and motioned for me to approach our adjoining fence. She invited me to her yard to visit.

"Can you read my palm?" "M" asked, shyly.

I said of course, promising it would be fun. We sat at a worn, round picnic table on her patio as I studied her small, frail palm.

She questioned, "Will I be alone for my remaining years? I'm seventy-five and I hate being without a partner."

I answered, "Your palm indicates many activities, new friends, involvement with groups at Church, but you will be alone."

She motioned for me to follow her inside the house. "I want to show you something," she said.

I walked into the immaculately kept ranch home. She guided me through the formal living room into the kitchen. "Look at this!" "M" exclaimed, pointing to the kitchen table. "I set out two dinner services every evening even though my husband is no longer here. I know it's a wrong behavior, but after forty years of living with my soul mate, I do it automatically. I talk to him daily too."

I asked, "Is your daughter aware you set two place settings every day? What does she think?"

"She thinks I'm a nutcase," she answered.

During the season's first snowfall "M" walked out to her mailbox and slipped, hitting her hip on the cement curb. It was a fluke of timing that I happened to be peering out my front room window precisely at that time. I ran outside to help her. She was in shock, unresponsive. I yelled for a neighbor to call 911 while I stayed with her until the paramedics arrived. She was in the hospital for ten days, having a pin inserted in her hip. Her daughter lived in a rural town north of us and was notified by the hospital about the accident. "M" recuperated at her daughter's house for four weeks. When she came home she was weak as she pushed her walker in front of her. She was delighted to be back among her familiar things. I offered to keep a neighborly eye on her, get the mail and bank for her until she was on her feet.

"You might as well be her other child," her daughter laughed, "I can't get down to Mom's except weekends. I'm a single mother with four kids and two dogs, living on a farmstead. I work like mad selling real estate. I'm so grateful you're next door."

It wasn't long until "M" bounced back. The walker put away, she began to do her own chores, looking more like herself every day. She drove to the bank where she usually used the drive-up window to do her banking, but that day she parked in the lot and walked into the bank where she conversed with the teller relating her accident. She withdrew several hundred dollars from her account. Putting the money in her purse, she returned to her car.

There were two young Hispanic men in line behind her who overheard the conversation. Ascertaining she lived alone they stepped out of the line and followed her. "M" was unaware she was being followed. The men drove their old car, following hers. As she approached her driveway she operated the garage door opener, then drove inside. Still stiff from her surgery, she emerged slowly from the car. The two men pulled up alongside her car in the garage. "M" doesn't recall how she ended up on the cement floor, but she remembers hearing the men talking as they emptied her purse and threw it on her back. She faked a faint; they left her there. Laying very still, eyes closed, she prayed silently they wouldn't kill her.

"The bag's out cold," one man said. "Let's check the house. They stepped over her small body and sauntered through the entryway leading into the house.

"M" visualized them deep inside the house, and then feeling somewhat safe, raced over to my house. "Quick, call the police!" she yelled through the closed door. "I just got mugged! The robbers are in my house right now!"

We notified the police of the robbery taking place, then hid behind my living room drapes, terrified. We watched as the police car coasted silently onto her driveway. When the thieves discovered a silent police car pulling into the driveway they dove through the back patio door, then jumped the six-foot chain link fence into my backyard. I had two yellow Labradors and a mixed breed dog. All three were sleeping in their den in the bushes next to the house, hidden from view. As the men landed in my yard the dogs went into a crazy, frenzied, protective attack mode, barking incessantly, chasing them in circles. One of the men dropped "M" 's wallet as he stuffed papers and bills into his coat pocket.

Meanwhile the police discovered two parked cars in the garage, and then proceeded to search the house. As they entered her all glass windowed family room they saw my three dogs chasing the men. Instantly realizing what had happened, they ran into "M" 's backyard. A creek ran along our backyards on the far side of the back fence. When the robbers hopped the fence they landed in the cold, rushing creek. The police waited in "M" 's yard, on the creek side of the fence, undetected. They handcuffed both men and took them into custody.

"M" gave the policemen a brief statement. "Who's removing that car from my garage?" she asked.

The police explained they had to check the license plates through headquarters to determine if the vehicle was stolen, then they would call to have it towed.

"M" asked me to help her search her house to see if it had been ransacked. Cautiously, we checked every closet, and drawer in the house and found that nothing was missing.

47

Satisfied her home was secure; "M" called her daughter. I remained with her until her daughter arrived.

"Thanks again for being there for Mom," she said tearfully. "Mom's lucky to have two of us watching over her."

#11 ENOUGH ALREADY: May 1981

I was involved in a Singles group in Indianapolis where I became acquainted with a middle-aged woman, "B". At a monthly meeting she requested a palm reading. We found a quiet spot that was private.

"What are my prospects for love?" she asked

Studying her palm I discovered she was complicated. A wealthy widow who had been happily married for fifteen years, her husband was killed in an auto accident. They had a twelve year old son. She remarried two years later, but it terminated in divorce after three months because of her bizarre behavior. I explained she would have to dispose of the tapes running in her head in order to meet new men. I told her she needed to focus on a goal and ground herself, to center with the earth in order to overcome the traumatic events she had experienced.

"Want to know why we divorced so quickly?" she questioned. She related her story. Because she believed her first husband and she were soul mates and loved him deeply she had been unable to forget him, even though remarried. Her second spouse was loving, giving and supportive. The sticky issue involved their lovemaking. She kept a tape recorder stashed under her side of the bed. Whenever the newly married couple attained a climax she reached down, pushed the play button on the recorder and her first husband's eulogy played. The new husband reacted in livid anger whenever she turned on the tape. He demanded she stop the abusive behavior. She agreed to stop using it, but continued playing it. He had no choice but to file for divorce.

"If you should be lucky enough to find a mate again, are you going to repeat that same sick behavior?" I inquired.

She answered, "I burned the tape the day I received my divorce papers from his attorney. I learned my lesson."

At our Singles group she met a widower, a retired chemist who had recently lost his wife. They dated six months, were compatible and happy together. They married and while on their honeymoon in Egypt he died from a heart attack. She brought him home and again had to go through the ordeal of a funeral. On that day, with a house full of guests, her teenage son decided to grill a hot dog. He dragged their barbecue grill through his bedroom window and set it up in his bedroom. After the majority of guests departed "B" walked down the hallway to check on her son whom she hadn't seen in several hours. She discovered him, as he lay dead in his room, sprawled across his bunk bed. He had died from carbon monoxide poisoning. Devastated, she threw her arms up and screamed "My God, why does everything have to happen to me. I'm a good person, please, I've had ENOUGH ALREADY!"

#12 SHE SAID "I DO" MANY TIMES: January 1982

Attending a Home Show Exhibition with my husband, we ran into a man who was formerly married to our old neighbor. He excitedly told us about his new wife, and then introduced us. She was a pretty redhead; we hit off a friendship immediately and talked easily as we strolled down the aisles looking at the fair booths. I found her interesting, full of pep and energy. We planned to meet for lunch to get to know each other better. While we had lunch she asked for a palm reading. Her hand revealed a history of two divorces prior to this marriage. Her first husband desired a younger woman.

She said sadly, "I gave that man the best years of my life. I entertained for him, helped him at work, ran a home and managed two young kids, then he dumped me."

I saw bitterness, aggravation and pain from the unwanted divorce in her hand. Fearful of being alone, she began dating and found "J", her second husband, two years her junior. She knew it was a mistake the day they married, but she couldn't stop herself. He treated her children with disgust, showing affection only for his son. He was angry all the time and spent a minimum time at home. Their lovemaking became non-existent. She felt their marriage was failing and approached him about a trial separation. He became violent and stabbed her in the shoulder with an ice pick. She told me she screamed and ran out of the house, leaving her two young children behind, the ice pick stuck in her shoulder. A neighbor rescued her and called the police.

"They had to call an ambulance," she said.

"What about the children?" I asked.

"They slept through the ordeal, thank goodness." "The police arrested him asleep in the recliner, blood on his hands and clothes."

Detained in a Psych ward for seventy-two hours, "S" had her attorney file for divorce. She signed papers to have him institutionalized. Once she got over the bad taste in her mouth, "S" again began to date and met husband number three, our friend. He had a ten year old son while she had an eleven year old daughter and a thirteen year old son. Theirs was a blended family. Looking at her hand I detected disaster in the future for the latest marriage but said nothing. A few months later they were divorced.

She called me, crying, "I'm never going out again! I can't find peace or happiness with a man! I'm thirty-two with three divorces already!"

I advised, "S", "Spend time alone, something you have never done. Experience life with no men. Work on yourself, reinvent you, stay busy and when the timing is right you will end up with "Mr. Right". There will be no bickering, criticism, complaining, competition or sexual tension. You will like and dislike the same things, react the same way. There will be total acceptance, a bonding of true love between you. You've never experienced a relationship like this. It will happen when it's supposed to happen. You must be patient."

#13 I DID WHAT I HAD TO DO: March 1983

I relocated to Santa Barbara California in the spring, 1983. My mother introduced me to her celebrated hairdresser, "J". He created high fashion styles for movie stars, the theatre and others of fame. He had been employed at the Mall by a prestigious department store for seven years when the police arrived one morning and removed him from the exclusive beauty salon handcuffed, in full view of his clients. The story circulated and was common knowledge that he had been ringing up only fifty percent of the shop sales and services, embezzling for several years. "J" deposited the pocketed money in a secret bank account called MAMM, making hefty weekly deposits. The account name was a code he devised using the first initial of each of his children's names. His oldest was Mary, the three boys, Arthur, Matt and Michael. After two years passed "J" was released from prison with the stipulation to repay the $150,000.00 he acquired illegally. Since he possessed the skill of master hairdresser he chose to re-enter the beauty field and made the decision to return to an area where his reputation as a stylist was known. He approached wealthy patrons who knew of his reputation and who were in favor of his continuing his career. "J" was gifted with a beautiful, fully outfitted; seven station beauty shop on a main street on the outskirts of Santa Barbara in a desirable location. Having listened to the gossip I was curious to meet "J". His appearance was disappointing because he looked ordinary, with dark, short cropped hair, horn-rimmed glasses and physically short in stature, a smallish man around forty.

I greeted him with a warm smile, "Mom told me quite a lot about you," I said. "I'm anxious to see what you can do to make me look spectacular."

He studied my facial features noting I resembled my mother. He questioned my lifestyle, how I wanted to look and how much time I was willing to devote to upkeep of my hair. I mentioned I was a palm reader and that I'd enjoy giving him a reading when he wasn't so snowed with clients.

"I'm booked solid," he replied. "I slave seventy hours a week."

"Where do you find the energy?" I asked. "What motivates you?"

"Didn't you hear," he said, "I have a huge debt to repay a department store and I have to earn enough to live on too."

We made an appointment for his reading the following Monday, his only blacked out day in the shop. That day he escorted me to an apartment across the alley, behind his shop. Holding his palm in my hand I picked up his energy and saw his life flash pictures in my mind. I felt the tension he had encountered in the past. Suddenly I realized why he broke the law.

"You siphoned money from the department store beauty shop to send to your family in West Virginia," I began. "They were totally dependent on your support and you felt an obligation to help."

He stared at me, amazed. Finally he replied, "Yes, my ex was involved in a wicked traffic accident. She's totally disabled and will never be able to work again. We have four children ranging in age from seven to twelve years old. I have to feed, clothe and educate all of them. Sighing, he said, "I figured out a way to send them money. I simply did what I had to do."

"Your family was distressed, suffering while you were in Santa Barbara working on famous, wealthy, people, and you felt terrible." I reported. "I believe the smell of big bucks swept you off your feet."

"You understand the whole scenario. I produced my own television show called "Beauty Is Only Skin Deep". I created many upbeat, beautiful styles in those days," he groaned.

I questioned, "What did you do while you were in prison?"

"Sitting in jail with no funds going home to my family nearly killed me. One day I found the solution to the problem and formulated a plan. While incarcerated I did some constructive thinking and invented my own line of cosmetic products. I decided to manufacture and market them in West Virginia so my ex-wife could oversee the business from her wheelchair. By setting up my business that way she'd constantly have income coming in to sustain the family. I located a few key people who believed in my abilities and was able to find backing for the project. They knew my concept would be profitable for them," he said. "In the end it proved to be my therapy."

"It sounds overwhelming," I said in awe.

"I admit it was difficult. I chose a name for my products, created a logo and dreamed up the combinations of ingredients for each one. I thought about catchy advertising and came up with the name JOICO. Daily, I contacted realtors in West Virginia requesting they search for a facility where I could set up the warehouse/factory business. The task was monumental, but I concentrated on results and eventually accomplished my goal," he smiled.

"I'm really impressed," I replied.

"Enough about my past," he said, "I want you to tell my fortune, what's going on now?"

I studied his Love line. "You married in your early twenties."

"With a baby on the way getting married was the right thing to do," he answered.

I remarked, "There were four live births in six years. Everything was going swimmingly until you quit your job in the coalmines to enroll in Beauty College. I feel resistance from your wife. She feared change and it frightened her. She resented your dreams and ambitions, growth in new directions."

"You hit that right! We were divorced because of it. She couldn't accept my entering the beauty industry," he answered.

I said, "You love your children very much but you couldn't be near them and earn the money you do in California. In West Virginia no one appreciates your gift."

"I hate going back. My ex hangs around when I want to spend time with the kids," he offered. "I send for them to come here, one at a time during school vacations. It's the only quality time I get to spend with them," he whispered.

"You seem to be happily involved with a lady," I suggested. "Her name begins with a "V". I think she is your soul mate."

He stared at me with a newfound respect. No one knew of this woman, a friendship-turned-love. He spent his days living a low profile lifestyle due to his tainted reputation. "Her name is Vicky," he supplied. "What do you see about our new relationship?"

"It's exciting and comfortable, great for both of you. She's fifteen years younger, and perfectly happy living out of the limelight. She prefers being alone with you," I announced.

"Right you are! We're compatible and meet on many levels, not just in the bedroom. We meld emotionally and mentally, and we love each other," he exhaled loudly.

"I see no marriage plans in the future. I see a solid relationship where you share everything," I explained.

"I will never marry again and Vicky accepts my philosophy on that. I married once and got trapped. I have to be a free agent," he said with a sure-fire opinion.

I explained he had good health, and that he was strong but he needed to cut down on the backbreaking pace at the shop or he would get ill. He thanked me for the insightful reading and suggested we walk back to the beauty salon.

"I'm very impressed with your palm reading ability, Myrna," he smiled. "This was my first palm reading. You actually uncovered the real me that I hide it from the public."

I was pleased with his compliments. He pulled out the number one chair and donned a smock.

"Sit down," he instructed, pointing at the chair. "I'm giving you a special complimentary full treatment. I'm creating a new style for you, one that befits a palmist of your caliber. I'm adding facial highlights. Enjoy the rest of the afternoon while I work my magic and pamper you."

#14 I LIVED THROUGH AN UNFORGETTABLE HELL: November 1983

Mother introduced me to her friends after I moved to Santa Barbara. Ruth was sitting under a hair dryer in "J" 's beauty shop. Her story profoundly touched me, making a lasting impression. The cosmetologist combed her out as we conversed. I discovered she was a Holocaust survivor who had married a German Jew and immigrated to America. She asked if I would read her palm when she was finished. We walked outside and sat on a bench by the door. She

55

recounted her life in Germany that had been lovely until the war broke out when she was fourteen years old. The nightmare that was her life lasted three terrible, prolonged years.

"Hitler robbed me of my adolescence," she cried. "Those dirty Nazis stole my youth, my health and they dehumanized me too. I've got nothing to show for those three years! Memories of my wasted girlhood in a God-forsaken concentration camp are traumas I shall never get over." She explained the anguish, torment, and inhuman treatment she endured. She related her two sisters and parents were sent to different camps while she was interred at Auschwitz. When Ruth learned the fate of her parents and sisters in the ovens from a fellow inmate she was shattered, left an orphan. Eyes glistening, she continued, "Nothing is worse than losing your entire family! I survived those dreadful years by carrying a picture of them in my mind's eye.

I prayed for them:

'May it be thy will, Lord our God and God of our fathers, to lead us in safety and direct our steps in safety; mayest thou bring us to our destination in life, happiness and peace. Deliver us from every enemy and danger on the road. May we obtain favor, kindness and love from thee and from all whom we meet. May the Lord bless you and protect you; may the Lord countenance you and be gracious to you; may the Lord favor you and grant you peace.' "

Changing the subject, I began, "Your food allotment was minimal. How did you survive?"

"We lived all day for the evening meal, the only time we were fed. Usually it was only a piece of stale bread and a tin can of weak vegetable soup. I never once saw so much as a vegetable in it," she said.

Looking at her palm, I remarked, " I see you went to sleep hungry most of the time. You were raised to be a polite child and never pushed or shoved to get to the front of the line, to grab the food first."

"There were ways to supplement the rations. Some of the older German guards were nice and took pity on the youngest children. They often smuggled bits and pieces of their food to us. If they got caught their punishment would have been severe. They took chances like that a few times a week," she related. They told us war was hell, not a fit place for school children."

I asked how she was able to live in such squalor, infested with lice, no soap and in the absence of protective heavy clothing during the harsh winter months. Shrugging her shoulders she recounted many did not live through the hardships imposed on them.

Ruth stated, "I am a very strong person. Watching the Germans snuff out the lives of so many Jewish citizens, I became hardened to it. I do have a recollection of a repulsive episode burned in my memory. I was selected for the digging crew in the potato fields and it was awful, backbreaking, difficult physical work all day long. I wasn't used to doing that kind of work but I did it to stay alive. We were instructed to dig long rows for planting. One day my shovel dug into the soft soil when the earth moved. I jumped, not knowing what made the soil move at the spot where I was working. A skinny arm protruded out of the dirt, then another. I stood mesmerized as I saw a leg roll out of the soil and a weak man slide out of the ground. He was emaciated, near death, mud in his hair and eyes. The incident unnerved me and I threw up. A few minutes later I pulled the shriveled man up on all fours, constantly watching the fields behind me the entire time for the nasty guards. I motioned for him to follow me on his hands and knees but he was too weak, unable to move. I crawled, dragging him on my back to the barbed wire fence by a cluster of dense trees where I propped his thin body against a tree. His watery eyes pleaded, soundlessly begging me for death. I looked away silently as I recited the prayer for the dead."

'Yisgaddal v' yiskaddash shmey rabboh,

B'Olmoh dee v"roh chir-usey V'yamlich malchusey, B'cha-yeychon uvyo-meychon Uvcha-yey d'chol beys yisro-eyl, Ba-agoloh uvizman koreev V'imru omeyn.'
In English I prayed:

'Be not afraid of sudden fear, neither of the desolation or the wicked, when it cometh. Take counsel together, and it shall come to nought; speak the word and it shall not stand; for God is with us.' He closed his dirt-filled eyes in peace. In that instant he was gone. I simply couldn't cry. I was too drained," she related.

Softly, I continued, "Ruth, you called on God many times to take your life. But I also see a strong will within you that would not give up."

Ruth replied, "I was raised an Orthodox Jew and I called upon my religious teachings. My inner strength to live through the ordeal came from God. After the war ended I lived in a cramped one-bedroom apartment in Austria with two young Jewish women, the only other teenage survivors from the camp. I met John, an extremely kind German Jew. He brought me gorgeous flowers with huge boxes of candy every Sunday and I was finally able to relax. John encouraged me to eat wholesome food and to sleep long hours. During that year we fell deeply in love. He asked me to make his life complete by marrying him. His proposal was bittersweet because I was distressed. I had no family to invite to the ceremony. My roommates said not to worry; they'd take care of everything. The girls invited the members of their families and friends who survived the camps, made my exquisite wedding gown, arranged for the flowers and organized the food. Our beautiful diminutive nuptials took place in June on a Saturday evening, after sundown where the Rabbi said a few words. It was a moving ceremony, with lively music, dancing and flowing wine," she said.

"I know you were a stunning bride," I announced.

"I shall always cherish those precious memories. Even though my family was absent, I believe in my heart they were present with us on that day," she said, tears in her eyes.

"From your hand, I see your soul mate John took you on an adventure as you traveled to America. He was hopeful for a fresh beginning for your new life together and knew the opportunities would be greater for you here," I offered.

"You are absolutely right," she beamed. "I most sincerely want to thank you from the bottom of my heart for taking the time to read my palm."

#15   DON'T LET LIFE PUSH YOU AROUND: March 1984

I was friendly with a Chinese woman who worked with me at a Water District in California. She was Head of Accounting while my responsibilities were under her in Accounts Payable. One day in my office, just hanging around she asked me to read her palm. I suggested we step over to the window where the light was bright. I considered her palm, mentally noting she ran herself ragged, engaging in too many extra curricular activities. Her husband had treated her badly, she was beginning to despise her job and her sleep patterns were disturbed.

"What can I help you with "A?" I inquired.

"I need to figure out my life," she cried. "Our twenty-fifth anniversary is soon and I got nobody celebrating with me! My husband is living away from home."

I told her sometimes bad things happen in all marriages. She didn't believe me.

"I need to find a way out of the mess my life is in," she stammered. "Help me!"

"A", I began, " concerning your job, a change would be wise. Why not discuss it with your Supervisor? Maybe you can transfer to a new position. Or, you can keep working and look for something away from the District."

She listened, making mental notes.

I started, "You are running around, out five nights a week."

"I go away five nights a week," she replied. "I take classes in ceramics and in photography and exercise at the Recreation Center. Friday nights I go dancing."

"What motivates you to run so hard?" I asked. "Why don't you go home after work?"

"I'm afraid, all alone and I'd rather keep busy when I'm not working. Staying home feels bad. I keep busy day and night," she sobbed. "I hate my son lately too, he bad mouths me all the time. I'm not taking that from him if I remove myself from in front of him. He can't pick fights with me if I'm not there. I feel better if I just go out. His Father could straighten him up but he's not around."

"How can I help you?" I questioned.

"I file for divorce soon. I will need good friends for support then. I'm not feeling strong. I must locate an attorney to handle my case but I can't force myself to search in the phone book for one. Can you be my strength?" she whispered.

"Are you positive your marriage is finished?" I inquired.

"He moved out three months ago and has not called once. He enjoys his Chinese man friends better than his own family. They gamble all night, playing Maj Jong. Nobody at the District guesses my problems; only you get it from my hand. This has been my private hell," she related.

"My suggestion is to stop pushing yourself so hard during the week. Go to the doctor and get medication if you have to, take care of yourself. You aren't eating properly either. If anything happens to you who would take care of your kids? Your son is hard on you because he feels abandoned by his father so he's taking it out on you," I explained. "You are a sweet, sensitive person who deserves happiness."

"A" seemed a little more at ease as she digested my advice.

She thanked me for being her friend and we hugged each other in my office.

#16   I NEVER GOT THE CHANCE TO SAY GOOD-BYE: January 1985

A tall, dark-haired woman was given my name as a reference for a palm reading. We met me at a luncheon when our mothers introduced us. She asked me to read her palm there. We retreated into the ladies room and sat on an overstuffed couch when I studied her hand.

I began, "You were married to a professional man but I see you are alone with two young children now. You've just moved in with your family. I feel you were a part of a tragedy that may have occurred thousands of miles away. It's what caused this move."

"True," she replied.

"I notice by your lines, you witnessed something so horrible you can hardly speak of it," I said.

"Again you are right," she nodded.

"I'm not describing an accident am I?" I questioned.

61

She shook her head no in response.

"I sense a group of four adults present . . . something happened," I offered.

She stiffened. "What do you see about the four of us?"

"To begin with, your Love line is intense. Yours was a happy, complete marriage. You stood beside your mate through high school, college and many years of higher education. There was never anyone else for either of you. A soul mate's magnetic thread held you together," I explained.

She supplied the information, "There was an incident . . . it happened so fast. We were out for dinner with our best friends, and then took a walk by the ocean in Miami. Someone mentioned going for dessert and everybody started talking about ice cream sundaes. We left the beach area in search of a treat. Two homeless guys mugged us. They demanded our money and jewelry. Three of us complied but my husband refused to give up his wedding ring, which angered the thieves. One of them pulled a gun from behind his back and stuck it on my husband's chest," she said sadly. "Suddenly we heard a muffled noise and he collapsed on the sidewalk, shot point blank through the heart."

"I'm so sorry," I said sympathetically. "Can you continue?"

"Our apartment was near the hospital where my husband was a staff doctor. In the summertime in Florida the heat gets oppressive. We often walked by the ocean to cool off with the breeze. I wish we hadn't that night, then I wouldn't be a widow," she exclaimed. "After the attack I went into shock. I don't remember anything else until I woke up in the hospital where I saw my mother, her new husband and our Rabbi standing next to my bed. I asked for my spouse. Everybody looked away, tears in their eyes. He was murdered right in front of me. I didn't even get the chance to say good-bye," she cried.

"I didn't want to make you re-live that event, but in order to project into your future I had to learn your past history," I explained.

She dabbed a hanky at her eyes. "What's going to happen to us?" she asked.

"You will heal one day," I said soothingly. "Time heals. There are stages of grieving you will have to experience in order to be whole again. You have family for support and guidance. You and the children will begin anew. You'll own your own home one-day and your children will grow up there."

She admitted she wanted her own home for the three of them and said she didn't want to live on top of family, but nearby.

"A new home, a new beginning," I sang out.

"Dependency on family isn't the solution to my dilemma is it?" she inquired.

"No, but you're where you need to be now. Your children need you to be a strong parent now. I see a second marriage for you in two or three years. Give yourself time."

She smiled through her tears and held my hand for a minute after we completed her reading.

#17 HE COULDN'T TAKE THE PAIN: October 1986

I worked with "P" at the City of Santa Barbara. He was a small man, rather good-looking, with a receding hairline, and the beginning of a paunch. I inquired about his tour of duty in the service.

He answered, "Read my palm. And you'll see where I'm at and what I lived through in Nam."

We met the following evening after work in a lovely city park by a cascading fountain. "I hope we don't lose the light until I've finished reading for you," I said. "I need

63

bright light to be able to see the lines on your hand". He sat quietly as I studied his hand.

"You were very shy as a youngster," I announced. "As you matured a new personality emerged. By sixth grade you were an incessant talker, secure in your crowd of peers." We discussed his three failed marriages, education and the upcoming trial for the rape of his teenage stepdaughter.

"What do you see for me now?" he inquired.

"I see that your last marriage was to a woman ten years older than you with three children, the oldest, a teenage girl. Your lines show a hard tour of duty in the Armed Forces," I explained.

He answered, "It was no picnic over there."

"After discharge your palm shows that you returned to your old familiar stomping grounds, the university. But when you arrived on campus life wasn't what you expected there. You felt like you were out of sync, out of touch with reality, unable to rekindle that warm, familiar feeling you remembered from years before. Instead you relived your war experiences every day and that is when you began drinking heavily," I reported.

"I tried desperately to find the path back. I was desperate to find a little bit of happiness. I even joined AA; it's where I met my third wife. She and I were a hot and heavy item, and after dating six months, we married. We were content, happy, except for one fly in the ointment; her daughter. She constantly came between us," he stated, sadly.

"What happened at home that finally pushed you over the edge?" I inquired.

He answered, "After a fairly long time, the step-daughter tattled to her mother, admitting I had bedded her. The truth was out in the open. At first I called her a bald-faced liar and denied all her accusations. Finally though, I confessed my guilt. That's when the shit hit the fan! I was thrown out of the house. It's been hell these past few weeks living out of the back of my camper truck."

"You appeared in court yesterday. What happened?" I asked.

"For once in my life I got lucky. The Judge was a good old soul who understood the stress and trauma of Nam," he replied. "Our playtime sex was by consent so he let me off with a stern warning about screwing around with under age partners. I'm not allowed to return to the house, ever. The divorce is a given," he explained.

I shook my head in sadness as I noted his hand revealed severe depression, a blackness surrounding him. As we completed his reading the sun dropped behind the mountains.

NOTE: The following week "P" 's suicide was reported in the Santa Barbara newspaper. He hadn't reported to work all week; none of his friends knew his whereabouts. He was camping in the foothills and on a moonless night he built a huge bonfire and threw himself into it. He left a note saying he gave up.

#18 THIS BOOK IS MY LIFE: April 1987

Working as a Senior Steno for the City of Santa Barbara I became friendly with a young black woman named "J" who changed her name to Sojourner.

"What does Sojourner mean?" I asked.

"One who travels," she replied. She explained her father was a Baptist Minister in South Carolina. She moved away from there because her soul mate enrolled in the renowned School of Photography in Santa Barbara. One day she showed up on his doorstep, announced she had arrived and that she was never going home. He lived in a rental house with five college men. She became their sixth roommate.

I baked a beautiful sheet cake to celebrate her birthday and took it to work. Everybody stopped by to sample the cake and congratulate her.

"Hey Myrna," she yelled across the room, "I know what I want for my birthday."

I was prepared to listen to a long request list when she asked for a palm reading session. We decided to do it after work when no one would be around the office. We discussed her family, dreams for the future and her fiancée. She asked direct questions and I answered them honestly.

"See this book?" she asked, holding up a leather-bound, zippered daytimer. "I want to share it with you. This book is my life. It has all my writing materials, letters, appointments and dreams for the future recorded in it."

We discussed her writing ability and ambitions. "You love to explore everything, learn as much as you can," I announced.

"I love to write about my experiences too," she replied. "I have a burning desire to accomplish so much in my lifetime. Do you see that on my hand? Will I write, produce and direct my own television show?"

"Why not? You can reach for the brass ring anytime. It only takes imagination and creative thought processes, both of which you are loaded," I said.

She explained, "I want to bring a ray of hope to the Afro-American women in our community. They are not as curious as I. I want to teach them life is to be lived, to join in society and to be free to go along life's path, wherever it takes them. I want them to want to go places they dared not enter before, and to help them lose the fear of the unknown. I recognize I'm a pioneer, but I believe God put me here to lead my people out of the depths," she exclaimed.

"That's lofty idealism. I admire you for it," I said.

#19   YOU WILL MEET A LOVELY WOMAN: October 1987

At a Water District in California my boss requested I read his palm. He had just finalized a troubled divorce, sold his home, won his ten-year-old son in a custody battle and relocated to a new townhome.

"I have a lot of issues," he began, "I don't know if you can sort them out or not."

I studied his light-complexioned hand. The lines carried a red hue, a signal he was loaded with a lot of anger. I explained the color of the lines represented anger and pain. He nodded.

"You got dumped and it hurt," I began. "You're better off now than you were before the divorce but your system hasn't caught up and realized it yet. When you discovered your ex was having a fling with a beach bum that was the tip of the iceberg. She was cheating and carrying on for years behind your back."

"I knew about it for a long time," he answered. "I put up with it to keep our family intact. Eventually I couldn't stand it anymore when our son got old enough to understand her behavior was wrong."

" I see many confrontations about her secretive life. She admitted there were many lovers. That's why the court made you the custodial parent," I stated.

"That's old history. I'm really interested in where I go from this point in my life," he said.

"You passed through several stages. First there was the denial, then the knowing and doing nothing, and then taking action. You're upset with yourself at this time. You have to get yourself past the anger so you can go forward but you're stuck. Why not get involved, do something you were always going to do one day. I suggest you begin some new activities, volunteer, or sign up for a class." "Once you get

67

involved in new avenues you will meet a lovely woman who will be your friend, then your best friend. You knew her in a previous life; she will be your soul mate. You'll cultivate her friendship and eventually will become lovers, " I predicted.

"Sounds like a plan I can handle," he smiled.

"Another issue is work," I began. "The load you're carrying is far too great for one person. Because of the situation at home you poured yourself into work, putting in a lot of overtime. If you continue at this pace you'll stress out and will be no good for your son." I suggested delegation of the responsibility and routine duties to people he felt were competent in our department.

"OK Madam Myrna. I shall heed your advice. What activities would you recommend for my non-working hours?" he asked.

"How about skiing?" I offered. "The long drive to the mountains will clear your thinking."

"That's something I always wanted to do! I can ski my heart out and maybe I'll meet someone on the slopes or in the Lodge," he smiled.

I laughed. "Perfect! Get out and about! You really do need it, you look like the last rose of summer. Getting away can only be beneficial. Your inner child needs time to unwind, to play and be free."

"Well," he grinned, "I admit your reading surprised me. You are very intuitive and insightful. You picked up all these facts by looking at my palm."

We shook hands and I returned to my desk outside his office door. I peaked through the glass and noticed he had a far-away, dreamy look in his eye, contemplating his next move.

#20 EXCHANGE STUDENT: September 1990

Our home was opened to exchange students who were attending the University of California in Santa Barbara. One of our students, a 28 year-old Japanese male had many friends who called or stopped by the house to visit. Our house felt like the United Nations. One afternoon he brought six Oriental friends home from school to lounge on the patio. When I arrived home from work I served cookies and iced tea. They spoke broken English, but mostly I heard a lot of nervous laughter. My boarder asked me to read their palms. I agreed. It was an unusual session because of the language barrier, but they understood most of what I said. Various reactions were exhibited. Some laughed, or pushed each other; some boys blushed, punched one another and sometimes cried as they experienced feelings of homesickness. I read for them at the picnic table on the patio. The students sat silently watching me, transfixed with large eyes. As they prepared to leave they each shook my hand and thanked me profusely, bowing. My student asked me to read his palm after everyone had cleared out.

"I must make dinner," I explained, "I worked all day then came home to your impromptu party, so I'll have to read your hand later."

He helped me clear the kitchen, anxious for his reading. "Please, will you read my palm? " he questioned. "I am hopeful you be finding the good life for me."

We sat at the dining room table while I studied his palm.

"Your Life line is very long. You're strong and healthy, will probably live to the high nineties, maybe even to one hundred. Do you have relatives who lived that long?" I inquired.

He replied, "Yes, two grandmama still living. One ninety-nine years old, other one hundred and one!"

"You are a determined, serious student. To enter the UCSB Student Exchange Program, it looks like you worked ten years saving the necessary funds," I said. "Nobody helped you. Your motivation was the desire to earn a business certificate."

"You correct Mrs. Myrna, I save long time for trip to American school. It was very difficult not spending my own money on good times with all my friends every day. But I never do it. I work two jobs every day ten years," he answered.

"You are self-taught, is that right? I see from your hand you went to the library and read a lot of books to master many subjects," I stated.

"I am hungry for knowledge. I read ten books a week. They know me at library," he grinned.

"What are you studying at school?" I inquired.

"I study for degree Business," he replied.

"Where do you see yourself five years from now?" I asked. "What opportunities do you want in the future?"

"My dream is open restaurant in my Japan - small town. I serve Japanese and American food for customers. A classy joint," he laughed.

"That's a wonderful idea," I said. "You will do well. Your Work line shows hard work ethic will reap success. You strive for the results you desire. You set goals and work hard."

"Family have much faith in my dream," he admitted. "They not have money but good thoughts and love me. They say I good cook, with strong abilities. School teaching me cooking tricks of trade and business."

He questioned, "What you see for me with the girls?"

His Love line was barren, showing no romantic experience. After age thirty he would meet and marry the woman of his dreams, his soul mate from a past life. "You have never had a girlfriend. You are a late bloomer. There's someone for you, a wonderful woman, also Japanese. You will love and support each other," I reported. "I see she will work alongside you in your new business venture too."

"Where will I meet this wonderful woman, America or Japan," he questioned.

"She lives in Japan. You will meet through a business connection," I replied. "You must begin going out with women, practicing for when she appears on the scene. You're to have some dating experience. There is a two-year window of time until you meet your soul mate. You are twenty-eight years old, but your mother carried you for nine months, so in reality, you are almost twenty-nine. I predict a marriage in thirty to thirty-first year of your life," I said.

"Thank you very much for palmistry. That was Oriental method too, I recognize. You made happy my friends this day. They feel welcome in your house and they all are liking you, but I am loving you!" he exclaimed. He hugged me hard and ran, red-faced to his room.

#21 CHICKEN WINGS: September 1991

I participated in an American Business Women's Association Round Table function in Denver, a luncheon seminar. The main entertainer was Chicken Wings, a respected, well-known radio personality in the area. He presented his program and conducted an audience participation game. I was chosen to go on the stage to demonstrate a ten-minute word game to the audience. While performing his routine with him I picked up an undercurrent from him. He had sauntered by my palm reading booth on the mezzanine that morning and he caught my eye. Upon ending his show several hundred women gave him a standing ovation.

71

He winked and said, "Follow me backstage a minute, will you?"

Stepping behind the velvet curtain, we walked down an unlit hallway to a costume storage room, backstage.

"Your presentation was excellent," I bubbled, "I usually get bored at lectures, but you had them listening the entire time."

"I get bored too, unless the audience can tune in to my brand of humor. I was "on" wasn't I? You sure helped me out," he said.

"Why did you ask me to come back here?" I questioned.

"If you're psychic you already know the answer," he laughed.

"You want your palm read," I replied.

"Yep," he smiled, "I hope you can you do it now. I have another speaking engagement in an hour. How long does it take?"

"I can do a mini reading," I answered, studying his palm. "You are an extrovert, but as a young boy you were painfully shy," I began. "I feel you are unattached, and would like to find someone you can relate to, who enjoys the same things you do. You don't want to be lonely, left out the rest of your life. No matter how busy your work schedule is, or how much responsibility you take on that special someone is missing. You are in need of companionship, a mate. Your palm shows a marriage at an early age that didn't work out. You got divorced about twelve years ago," I offered.

"Yes, I agree it's been a long time to be alone. I've been in numerous relationships since the divorce but never "THE" one. You're absolutely right! I do want a partner. Will I ever find my soul mate?" he questioned.

"There is someone waiting in the wings for you but not in Denver," I predicted.

"Strange you're bringing that up," he mused, "I'm planning a Caribbean vacation next month. Will I find her then?"

"No, you'll meet when you're traveling. She'll be involved in the entertainment field and you will have that in common. You could meet her while waiting in an airport lobby or on a tour bus," I answered.

"Now I'm really curious." He inquired, "Should I cancel next month's trip?"

I replied, "No, continue with your plans. Don't walk around with unrealistic expectations of whom you might meet on vacation. You have to keep an open mind at all times though. A new business opportunity will be forthcoming and she may be in the big picture. Business trips in the future are important for you and that may have some relation to the chance meeting of your soul mate."

He thanked me for his reading. I suggested he not call me at 2:00 AM if he fell in love and felt the urge to share the news.

#22 I'D JUST AS SOON KILL YOU AS LOOK AT YOU: October 1992

My hair stylist in Indianapolis, "I" worked out of her home. One day as we waited for the color to process on my hair she nonchalantly asked me to read her palm. I held her hand in mine and discovered revealing and surprising facts. I asked her if her marriage was in trouble.

"Yes," she wept, "I can't get through to my husband anymore!"

I asked if they were communicating. Her reply was a tearful shake of the head, 'No.'

"Do you trust him?" I inquired.

"I thought I did, but not anymore," she answered sadly.

I noticed he was cheating on her as I looked into her hand. "I" felt it was possible, but denied it. They had three beautiful children, one daughter, married, one in college and a son in the fourth grade.

"I'd leave him but he has to help me get the kids raised and run the house," she sighed. "I can't handle this load."

I explained she was a strong person and should give herself credit. I said she could have any man she wanted. "I" is a natural beauty, a Dolly Parton look-alike without conceit or attitude. She worked long hours at her beauty salon then cleaned houses on the weekends to pick up extra money.

With a deep breath I said, "You should consider living on your own with the children. Project into the future - where do you see yourself in the next few years."

"I" looked into my eyes deeply, faced the facts and began to cry.

I said, "I believe people can be married but not be in a partnership. Your marriage is in name only. A person can be married and still be lonely. You're alone even when he's home aren't you? People get along fairly well once they separate. With the support of family and friends you can make it. It's time for you to take charge of YOU."

She listened intently as I explained the attraction individuals have for each other. I began, "Likes attract and opposites attract. You and your husband are opposites, plus he's entering the mid-life crisis and he's terribly restless. He isn't aging gracefully; instead he's searching for his lost youth by running around with younger women to prove to himself he's still desirable. If he's distant it's because he doesn't like being here right now."

74

"What will I do?" she sobbed.

I answered in a calm voice, "He could continue on this path and grow even more distracted until he finds someone to have a hot relationship with, or he may settle down, come to his senses and go back to being his old self."

I didn't hear from "I" for several months. When I dropped in for my quarterly hair appointment "I" was all smiles, singing.

"What's happening with you?" I asked.

"I got myself a boyfriend," she grinned. "A doctor I clean house for. He's a little older than I am, a wonderful man. He appreciates anything I do or say."

I asked if they were dating.

"I" was thoughtful for a minute. "We enjoy each other's company. He takes me out to dinner or a show every few days. I guess that's dating."

I asked how she arranged a social life since she and her husband shared the same house.

"He moved out awhile ago," she offered. "He lives with his latest girlfriend who is twenty-nine or so. She owns a rinky-dink home in a small farm town north of here. You were right on when you pegged him searching for his lost youth. I came to a decision the last time you were here when you advised me to get a life. You told me that I deserved one. When the golden opportunity presented itself I went for it. My weekend cleaning job was for the doctor. Usually he wasn't home when I went there, but that day he was. I needed some excitement and fun in my life. I was in the mood for his advances. He paid a lot of attention to me and we had such a good afternoon too."

I moved to California and lost track of "I" for several years. In town on vacation, I called her. "I" suggested I drop by promising a juicy tale to share. We sat over a cup of coffee as she poured her heart out, describing the car accident her spouse encountered on an ice slick road. His four-wheel drive vehicle hit a bridge abutment, bounced into a ravine, landing upside down in the drainage ditch. Trapped in the car for four hours, the steering column crushed his sternum. Given a 10% chance of survival he was in intensive care for eleven days. "I" sat at his bedside praying he would make it through the ordeal. When he was moved to a private room they were able to converse.

He stuttered, "I, I, I've reached a decision, I want to come home."

They talked non-stop for hours. When he was released "I" drove him to his girlfriend's house to pack his belongings. When he got home he looked into the eyes of his children and had to justify his childish behavior.

He accepted "I" on her terms. One day after his release "I" confided to him about her new boyfriend, the doctor. He couldn't accept her infidelity even though he had been unfaithful for several years. They argued constantly. He was on a six-month disability from work, underfoot, in her beauty shop daily. He embarrassed "I" in front of her clients; she lost some of them because they wouldn't tolerate his antics. Finally, "I" informed him their arrangement wasn't working, that he would have to leave. She explained his acting out was worse than his not being there for the family. He was shocked by her outburst. He didn't think "I" understood their situation. Screaming, he demanded to know where she thought he should go.

"I can't work for five more months," he whined.

"You should have put aside a nest egg during the time you lived with those stupid girls," she answered. "I learned how to live on my own. It wasn't easy. With no word from you, no financial help whatsoever, no contact with the kids, I nearly lost my mind!"

He had a temper tantrum and threw a lamp breaking the picture window in the family room. She hissed, "If you think I'm going to stand for this kind of behavior from you, you have another think coming. I'm calling 911 to report a domestic disturbance right now."

"You better be good with your story to the cops babe," he snarled, "I have the goods on you and the doc."

"I" turned her back on him and stalked into the kitchen. He followed and threw her body against the refrigerator. "I'd just as soon kill you as look at you," he spat at her.

"I" remained calm as she related her story. I noticed she still occupied her beautiful ranch home with the pool. I noted her thriving beauty business and the children who looked healthy and happy.

"Where is he now?" I inquired.

"He moved out that night right after that awful fight. He wouldn't talk to the police when they got here. I haven't laid eyes on him in two years. I just got my final divorce papers last week. My friend the doctor is still in our lives too. My girls like him very much and my son adores him. In fact, he's leaning toward medicine in a career choice because of him. We date every week. Marriage hasn't been discussed, but in my heart of hearts I know we will join together one day because we are true soul mates."

#23   THE MARRIAGE YOU SHOULD HAVE HAD IN THE FIRST PLACE: June 1993

Upon moving to Colorado we joined the Newcomer's Club. I anticipated the outings planned for the club on a monthly schedule. A hayride was arranged for the Keystone Resort. It was expensive but everyone thought it was worth the fee. The group encountered the tour guide at the hotel, bundled in winter clothes. We traveled to the mountain resort on a bus, and then took a second one to the area where the wagon-loading shack was located, halfway up the mountain.

77

Everyone covered up with the sheepskin blankets provided and huddled together, talking in hushed tones. Three fully loaded wagons pulled by double teams of workhorses plodded up the snow covered, steep path. Everyone disembarked at tree line. A huge log cabin stood in the moonlight. We were escorted inside where everyone gathered around the huge stone fireplace hearth. It was suggested that I read palms while we waited to be served the home-cooked dinner.

A man from our group approached and requested I read his palm away from the crowd so no one could eavesdrop. I agreed. We stepped into the well-lighted kitchen and sat on high barrels at the far end of the room. I placed my hand over his, feeling a shift in his energy. I realized he was not the man he said he was after all. His wife was a vivacious blonde woman in her late forties, charming and full of personality. She wore a full-length fur coat, matching hat, designer boots and soft leather gloves. He was tall, in his late fifties, moody. He wore a ski jacket, gray flannel slacks, a knit hat.

I asked, "Have you been married before?"

He answered 'No' emphatically, however, the Love line on his hand showed three previous connections, each a union in marriage. I began "I believe you have been involved in three meaningful relationships. I see three divorces on your hand."

His face twitched, he eyes grew hard and his hand stiffened in mine. "You aren't a fake! You really see the past in a palm," he said in awe.

I explained the wishbone markings represented relationships he had been involved in over the years. His hand carried four of them. "The line's on a palm are a record of one's life," I explained. "There was an exchange of money in the dissolution of each marriage. You were the receiving party in every broken romance. You asked for and got monetary compensation."

"What 's that prove? Why are you bringing finances up?" he asked.

"You want to learn about the relationship you are presently in or you wouldn't have asked me to read you privately," I said.

He laughed, "You really got my number! What's going on with the present wife?"

Noticing his Love line I saw he had found happiness for the first time in his life and would be content to stay with this woman forever. She was his soul mate. "This is the union you should have had in the first place," I reported. "You'll keep it together as long as you work at the relationship."

He thanked me for the reading and said he'd appreciate it if I didn't reveal personal information to anyone.

"Of course," I answered, "I never discuss anyone's reading. This is client privilege and I always respect that."

#24   BLACK CLOUD HANGING OVER HIS LIFE FORCE: April 1994

A singles group in Denver sponsored by a religious organization coordinates a dating service by keeping notebooks containing all the member's pictures with their written biographies in the library. Referred to as "The Book," participants send postcards to people who appeal to them with phone calls following. I was browsing through the numerous men's books when I became acquainted with a nice looking man in his late thirties who was sitting there going through the women's books. He asked my opinion on his fact sheet that was displayed in "The Book". He said he had received no postcards or phone calls from any of the women in the dating system and he wondered why. The remarks provided on his sheet were neat and well written, but his picture drew my attention as I placed both hands on it. An eerie feeling of death overcame me. I asked, "Have you ever been married?"

He replied, "Three times."

Curious to learn what caused three relationships to fail, I continued, "Were they younger than you?"

He replied, "One was my age, one a bit younger, the last one was ten years older."

I inquired, "Did you meet them through this dating service?"

He answered, "No, I found them myself. You won't believe this but all three of them fell down my basement steps and died."

He noticed my puzzlement and suggested I read his palm. I agreed, eager to see what information I could pick up from his hand. We moved to a corner of the library, out of the flow of traffic as I quietly contemplated his hand. He mentioned the police were satisfied all three of the deaths were accidental.

"Why are you seeking dates or another potential mate? With three bad experiences, how can you even bear to date again?" I asked.

He explained, "Nothing was my fault. I'm lonely and I need someone in my life."

I took an intense look at his Love line and noticed he used to be energetic, athletic, fun loving. He chose his first beloved at age twenty; they were the same age and had a two-year engagement. Six months after their marriage the first accident occurred. She broke her neck in the fall down the stairs and died instantly. He mourned for over a year, and then came out of the depression. Two years later he remarried, to a teacher at the neighborhood high school. On the eve of their first anniversary she slipped backwards, down the basement steps. She died in the ambulance on the way to the hospital. He spent the following year alone, grieving. For ten years from twenty-four to thirty-four he dated no one, became a recluse and simply went to work, then home every day. He met a woman, ten years his senior; they dated six months, and then planned to wed. Six weeks after the honeymoon tragedy struck. She too ended up at the bottom of the stairs, in the basement, dead. In every case the police were notified and accident reports were written. The basement steps were checked and rechecked, evidence gathered. It was suggested he sell his home and start fresh but he refused. Now he sat with "The Book" on his lap. He had high expectations of meeting yet another lady, one compatible with him, who would share his interests and his life.

"Nobody will go out with me," he complained. "I'm fairly good-looking and I hold down a pretty good job. I guess it's my reputation of three women's deaths in my home that scares everybody."

I told him he carried a detectable black cloud surrounding his life force. He asked for my advice and wondered what he could do to get a woman interested in him. I noticed he was depressed, had lost forty pounds over the past few years, and was no longer athletic. With nothing to look forward to, no excitement; his personal life was shattered.

#25 SAILBOATS: March 1996

While sitting in the front window of a beauty salon in Louisville Colorado reading palms, I met their product representative. She requested a reading.

"All I meet are women or gay men," she lamented. "What can I do? I'm thirty-five years old, a single Mom with

81

a first-grader and zero prospects in sight. I'm so needy! Help me please."

I asked what she did when she wasn't working. She replied she spent every free minute doing things with her son.

"No wonder you haven't met any eligible bachelors," I exclaimed with understanding. "You need to get out alone once in awhile. No man is going to ring your doorbell and announce, "I'm here!" You have to take risks in order to gain in this world. Why not try something new? You might be pleasantly surprised."

She asked me what she could do that would attract men to her.

I began, "Everyone has an inner child within. Your inner child is blocked because of the responsibility you took on since your divorce. You have guilt feelings if you don't spend every waking minute with your son. Since you're the sole wage earner and provider, you don't think of yourself. Everyone needs some diversion, a break in his or her daily routine now and again. Can you hire a babysitter for an hour a week and treat yourself to an activity?"

She listened to me and thought about a sitter.

"Maybe I could arrange to get away every so often," she answered.

"Your inner child needs the freedom to play. You never have any fun. You should just act silly occasionally then your inner child will be released," I explained. "Can you think of anything you never got a chance to do as a child? Maybe it was horseback riding or taking a photography class."

"I take my son to Cherry Creek Reservoir weekly where he floats his sailboat. I never did that when I was a kid. I'd love to float a boat," she said, excitedly.

I replied, "Your homework is to buy a sailboat for yourself and keep it hidden in the car. Hire a sitter and take your new toy to the Reservoir. Give yourself permission to be that little kid again. Float your boat and see what happens."

She thanked me for her reading, packed up her order books and left.

A month later she returned to the shop to restock their supplies. We smiled at one another. She looked like she had swallowed a canary.

"You'll never guess what happened," she announced. "I hired a sitter, bought myself a sailboat and hid it in the car. I went to the Reservoir and floated my boat. I felt great, so free that I started singing, sunning myself and I really enjoyed letting my little girl play. You were so right about that!"

She told me about a stranger who walked past her several times, then asked what she was doing. She explained her inner child; the little girl was floating her boat. He sat down next to her on the beach, took a sailboat out of his gym bag and unwound the string. They sat and floated their boats for four hours, talking, laughing like kids. At the day's end he asked for her phone number. "We've been dating every night since then. He cottoned to my child too. Can you believe it? I could hardly wait until my route to this shop was due so I could share the news with you."

She admitted her life needed a new direction. It put a new slant on her perspective. "Guess what else? The three of us float boats every Sunday and we have a ball!" she offered.

"I would like to see your palm once more," I said. I saw a soul mate mark; it was deep red. I knew it designated him as the ONE for her. "I think this is the relationship for the rest of your life," I predicted.

She thanked me for her second look-see and left on her route. Six months passed and either I missed her at the shop or they were no longer on her list. I received a wedding invitation at Christmas time from them. I was unable to attend the wedding because I was out of town; I heard it was a beautiful ceremony. Some time later she dropped by the shop with their wedding album. The pictures were delightful, but the one I loved was of the three-tiered wedding cake flanked with two well-used red sailboats flanking it.

#26 MURDER IN THE SUBURBS: May 1996

I volunteered to work at a dinner dance as a palmist for the American Business Women's Association when I encountered a woman whose story tore at my heart. She requested I leave nothing out and tell her whatever I saw. I noted she was the mother of a teenage son, she was an Office Manager and they lived alone. Five years earlier her family life was crushed when a bloody crime was committed.

"What kind of crime are you talking about?" she asked.

"I visualize a grown man laying face down in a pool of his own blood on the kitchen floor in a ranch house in the suburbs," I replied.

"Can you tell who was responsible?" she inquired.

"There's a history of physical abuse by your husband to both you and your son, who is developmentally disabled," I began. "You walked into the house after work, through the garage door. It was dinnertime; your son was doing homework at the kitchen table. The front door flew open with a fury by a raging male, angry because his dinner wasn't on the table. He scattered the boy's books all over the room, then beat him," I stated matter-of-factly. "He took turns beating both of you, screaming, ranting and raving. The abusive pattern was established long ago. That night something inside of you said "NO MORE" and made you fight back. On top of your son on the floor, he proceeded to choke him. I see you grabbed a butcher knife from the kitchen counter and stabbed him repeatedly to force him to release your son."

She stared at me in disbelief, breathing heavily, "I can't believe you saw that entire scenario so vividly on my palm. That's exactly what happened."

I went on to relate that she pulled her husband off the child and called the police. She nodded in agreement. Alive when they transported him to the hospital, he died on the operating table. She asked if I had read about the incident in the local newspapers or if I had seen it on television. I replied I didn't live in this state at that time.

"You got every miserable detail accurately!" she said. We sat together in silence momentarily, and then she questioned me. "Where am I today?"

I began, "Return in your mind to five years ago. Your son was taken from you by Social Services during the inquiry into the death of your spouse. The police files contained numerous reports and complaints regarding his behavior during loud domestic disturbances. Several neighbors filed complaints against him over the years. After the funeral you were detained in police custody for nearly six months, then finally released."

"Right, right, right!" she exclaimed.

"You held on to your job at the Dental Clinic, sold the home in the suburbs and moved to a surrounding town. You visit your son in Pueblo Colorado, where he was placed in a foster home as often as you can," I related. "You put your life back on track. Today you are free, dating, making new friends. Your true friends stood by you through the turmoil and they are still here. You feel fortunate to have such a wonderful, loyal support system. You have strength and peace of mind now. You're looking forward to bringing your son home and you are hopeful for the future."

We hugged, tears slipping down her face. Mine too.

I received a phone call from a man with a bubbly personality who wanted to book a palm reading appointment. My six month old yellow Labrador greeted "G". He informed me he bred labs. We went to the room where I conduct readings. I held his palm in mine for a moment reading his psychic heel. I picked up martial problems.

"I inquired, "How are things going at home for you?"

Stiffening, he stared at me harshly. "We just celebrated our twenty-fifth anniversary."

His vibrations spoke volumes to me. I felt pain, suffering, restlessness, anger and the need for more excitement in his life. I told him so. The grin on his face answered affirmatively. He explained he owned a sanitary cleaning service for commercial accounts and had been running it along with the lab-breeding farm for ten years. Boredom with work and no interaction with his wife made him search for other avenues to fill his time. He said he needed to taste new things, experiment, and find a challenge in his personal goals. He said he needed stimulation.

"What kind of business should I look into?" he inquired. "I'm selling the sanitary supply company."

Nothing gave me a clue to his interests. I could not feel work that would provide change, charge his energy and provide business success. I related that information and he admitted he desired to retire but felt it was premature since he was fifty-eight years old. He said he re-established an acquaintance with a past secretary, who was twenty-eight years old, explaining being with her, talking to her made him feel lively, alert and more appreciative of all females.

I asked him why he met his ex-secretary at noon three times a week in motels around town.

He laughed, "You're good, but wrong! We don't meet three times a week at noon in various motels. We go at it four times a week! I pay for three; she pays the tab for the fourth time. Pretty sweet deal isn't it?"

I felt he was fighting with himself with guilt because of the nooners, but I didn't discuss it.

He began, "I can't leave my wife because she's physically ill. She's weak, depressed and unresponsive. She isn't there for me anymore, but our home, those entire years together have to stand for something. I can't leave her when she's so dependent on me. I had to seek outside entertainment or go out of my gourd. I return home every night to a shell of a woman."

#28 MYSTERY WOMAN: August 1996

I was a guest on the popular early morning drive to work radio talk show in 1996, KTLK Denver Colorado. Once on the air I discovered the celebrity host was skeptical of psychics. Arms folded across his chest, he spoke harshly, "You'll have to reveal an event that's really spectacular before I become a believer."

The day prior to the show I requested thirteen radio personalities hand prints, Xeroxed. I studied each one recording pertinent facts on the back of each labeled sheet. I planned to pull each sheet as I met each celebrity, having it for insurance since I would be conducting his or her readings live, on the air.

Mike R., a radio and newspaper commentator was the first person I read. As he approached I noticed his hand; it was rather small, almost petite. His sheet indicated a huge, almost bear-like paw. I asked, "Is this your palm print?"

Both men snickered. "No, we were just having fun with you, that's another guy's hand," they both replied. They said they used it to test me to determine if I was a fake. My temper erupted; I threw all the papers in the air. (In broadcast the only thing never wanted over the airwaves is rustling paper by a microphone.) All eyes were on me, both outside and inside the booth.

The reading began. I noticed that Mike R.'s outstretched palm denoted personality traits of stubbornness, intelligence, a teacher's ability, a quick study type of mind, and a person who presented a façade to the world. I mentioned a woman he lived with for seven or eight years who wanted to marry him. I felt restlessness from his vibrations. I stated her name started with the letter "J" and that it was either Jenny or Jane. He supplied the information: her name was Jennifer, but her nickname was Jen.

The host asked me to tell them something only the two them knew, off air. The show broke for traffic. I prayed silently, selfishly calling on my angels for brilliance and expertise. During the next few minutes I forgot my nervousness, lost all awareness and re-entered his reading. An angel was perched on my right shoulder and whispered into my ear as I described an incident Mike R. was involved in with details. He sat motionless, a smile frozen on his face as I described a seminar he attended in S. Carolina for two work-related weeks, where he met an attractive woman. They immediately hit it off. I explained she had waist length hair, unusual for a woman in her forties. I described the two pearl barrettes she wore in her light brown hair, discussed her size and personality. I also said she was in the process of divorce.

Mike R., the smile gone from his face, inquired, "What if I did meet this mystery woman? What else can you tell us?"

I explained that upon leaving Denver he decided to lose his abrupt personality and act mild-mannered, quiet, giving, generous, different from his persona in Denver, compassionate, a caring individual. His interest peaked.

He replied, "I left town, going where no one knew me. I decided to re-invent myself. You are right about that."

I informed them the woman had two teenage sons and she was upset because her husband left them several months prior. The boys were home alone so she could attend the seminar for her job.

"She had beautiful green eyes except at night when she removed her contacts, then they were gray," I reported.

Hearing that detail, Mike R. leapt out of the chair and ran around the desk where he and the celebrity host hugged one another, patting each other on the back. "I don't feel too well," Mike R. stammered. His hands shook, he was pale, breathing irregularly. He held his forehead with one hand and his stomach with the other. "I'm going to my office to lie down. Bring Myrna Lou down when she's finished with your show. We have to talk."

#29 AT TIMES YOU CAN'T SEE THE FOREST FOR THE TREES: September 1997

One Saturday morning a gentleman and three co-workers, all women, arrived for readings. I read the women first, tape-recording their sessions. Those not being read sat in my family room entertaining themselves. When I stepped out after three sessions I discovered them spreading out a picnic on my coffee table, drinking wine coolers, playing cards and listening to mellow music.

When "M" came in I noticed his tan and beautiful silver hair immediately. He was over six feet tall, well dressed, and possessed a gentlemanly manner. I'm sixty years old, an old fart. I enjoy the company of women in their forties as you can see by the company I keep," he said.

I studied his hand under the light. The lines were well defined. He was light complexioned, but I could see his lines clearly. "You aren't a stubborn man." I explained, "I believe you have a lot of drive and determination. When you say you're going to accomplish something, it gets done." I noticed his Love line. It showed he had been in two marriages. He was lonely. The first union lasted twenty-four to twenty-five years and they produced three offspring. She suffered with an illness and lingered for four pain-filled years before she died. They were a team, soul mates in body, mind and spirit. He couldn't go out for over a year after his loss. When he began socializing again he met a woman ten years his junior who fascinated him. Pretty, witty, intelligent, she was full of life. They dated two years, and then married.

I asked, "Were you happily married to her?"

He replied, "Everything went well for us in those first years, then her personality changed completely. Her spending habits escalated, she had temper tantrums, headaches and at times was forgetful." He noted they lived under the same roof, but weren't partners. After five years of marriage he filed for divorce. The doctor told "M" his wife was a manic- depressive. At age fifty her mental condition began to deteriorate and her sex drive was non-existent. There was no communication. He needed the freedom from the strain of another wife's illness. "M" was living in his house with a non-responsive mate, lonesome, feeling alone. His hand didn't record a divorce at five years.

I stated, "You didn't go through with the divorce."

"I didn't have the heart to do it and I withdrew the papers," he admitted. "She promised she would seek professional help for her condition and of course, I like the fool, believed her." He knew they weren't compatible on any level but gave their marriage a second chance. Instead of reacting to his kindness she retreated into her own world. He continued, "I was beginning to believe she was sick because of me. I couldn't let her exist with no support, no income, so I stuck it out for two additional long years. We were both miserable. Her doctor said I wasn't to blame but . . ."

"You were married to her seven years?" I questioned.

He replied, "Sadly, yes. Life would have been much easier had I left that first time. Things got out of hand near the end. She was confused, disoriented. She slept all day then stayed up all night. While I was sleeping she built a huge fire in the living room fireplace but it was mid-July. Because I had the damper closed the house filled up with tons of black, heavy smoke. Thank G-d for smoke alarms. Another time she pasted pictures cut out of magazines all over the dining room walls. I asked her why she did it but she never answered. I returned home from work one evening and discovered bullet holes in every single picture on that wall. Literally, she destroyed our dining room."

"So eventually you left wife number two?" I asked.

"My attorney said it was useless to keep beating a dead horse, so I finally left," he offered. "A few months after I left she committed suicide. No one discovered the body for weeks."

I noticed several failed relationships on his hand since then and mentioned them.

"I was afraid of getting trapped again. I found fault or picked at every woman I dated until she finally asked me not to call, he answered. "I set myself up for failure, self-sabotaged every time."

"You seem to have no trouble surrounding yourself with the opposite sex," I commented.

"M" began, "I heard you on the Boyles AM radio show a few weeks ago. I knew you could relate to me. Your voice had a calming effect on me. I knew an appointment for a palm reading would help me get over the destructive behaviors I've been exhibiting. You are a genuine woman and I gravitate towards people who are "true blue" like you."

I thanked him for the compliments and searched his Work line. "How's your career?" I asked.

He replied, "A week ago my company downsized. I found myself out of a job at Merrill Lynch. It happened to me two days after my sixtieth birthday. Can you believe it?

They had my expertise for seventeen years. I'm more knowledgeable than my boss is, but they gave me my marching papers anyway. I'm regrouping to see what's available out there."

"Your Work line shows potential you haven't touched yet," I began. "I visualize you in your own business, run out of the house, consulting."

"What a wonderful shot in the arm you are! My possibilities are limitless! I'll purchase a computer and run my own programs on it. I can consult from a home office. Thanks for the smart advice. There are times one doesn't see the forest for the trees," he cried in relief.

#30 THANK GOD SHE STAYED HOME: October 1997

I received a phone call from a foreign man, "H", who said a friend of his wife's at work had heard me on a radio show. We met after the holidays when he advised me he was involved in several unrelated businesses and wanted direction. He was planning a start-up in a new venture and needed confirmation before investing heavily in it. He was a Publisher.

I held his palm in mine and felt his energy. I conducted the Psychic Vibration Test to see which way he was leaning. I also studied his handwriting for clues.

"Can you do for me, a complete comprehensive reading?" he asked.

"I'll read you and at the end should you have further questions regarding your business ventures we can discuss them," I answered. I talked about the five basic lines on a palm, the Life line, Love line and soul mate mark, the Work line, Reproduction lines and the Bracelets. I saw he had a full life, was happy in his marriage and that his work was rewarding, successful. He said he was on the Board of Directors at their Church and was socially accepted by everyone there. I explained his Life line showed he would live past the age of ninety. He came from a strong heritage. He offered information his parents were over that age and still going strong. He was born in Holland. He told me his health had always been fantastic. He was fifty-nine years old. His Work line showed he had already participated in seven different businesses previously. Success showed in business at his sixty-year mark. His Reproduction line was barren. We discussed his marriage with a soul mate from a past life. They shared many past experiences together that made their current relationship great.

"You have 100% support for each other, total acceptance. Your feelings run deep. You never worry about her being unfaithful and she never worries over you either," I announced.

"H" was uncommunicative, allowing me to do the talking as he listened intently. I uncovered his history, telling him he was a worrier as a young man because his Bracelets were full of loops. He let go of some of the inner tension when he was twenty-five. I asked if I missed anything, or if he had any questions.

"No questions," he replied. "I simply must say that was an honest, down to earth reading like nothing else I have ever encountered. It was so stimulating! Your reading was more intense than any I have ever had. You were right on every point! The palmistry class my wife and I took was nothing compared to your interpretation. I want to sign up to take your next class."

"H" later called for an appointment for his wife. When I read her I saw immediately that they were mirror images of each other, true soul mates. She enjoyed her reading as he sat quietly, smiling throughout the hour. They thanked me and we said good-bye.

The next day I received a disturbing phone call from him. He described a terrible ordeal and wanted to share the "gory" details. He drove to a nearby mountain town on business and asked his wife to accompany him. She was unable to take off work on short notice so "H" traveled alone. On the way home he encountered a freak accident on the frontage road. Had his wife been with him she would have been in the passenger seat of their car where a boulder the size of a refrigerator crashed into his car. "H" swerved to get out of the boulder's path. It would have hit the windshield, but instead took out the passenger side of the car. "H" lost control and flipped into the ditch. Cars driving behind him saw the accident and notified authorities. Police and Fire Rescue were called to the scene and used the Jaws of Life to extract him. His vehicle was totaled.

#31 I'M TOO YOUNG TO GIVE UP ON LIFE: November 1998

I worked as a Palmist for a Boulder Hospice Benefit on campus at the University of Colorado where I read the palms for over fifty participants in a smoke-filled, loud, crowded atmosphere. One of the men I read was quite impressed with my reading of his past. He was a sharp looking, older, distinguished, gentleman with silver hair in his late sixties. He stood six feet tall and had sparkling blue eyes. He told me he was deeply concerned. He had an issue with a remarriage in the near future. He had been a widower for eight months. He said this was his first time out, socially.

"I'm too young at sixty-seven to give up on life," he remarked.

I told him he had a full life with many pleasures and obligations that filled his hours. Even though he had family and friends around him it wasn't enough to satisfy him. He was a doctor and wasn't ready to retire yet.

"I've been corresponding with a pen pal," he admitted. "A woman in Prague who interests me. Do you have any suggestions on how we can get together?"

I asked if he had vacation plans. He informed me he was taking the month of December off. His other doctors would cover his patients.

"Why not travel to Europe in December? You could write your lady friend and let her know you'll be available during a portion of the trip," I suggested.

"What an obvious solution to this problem!" he replied, laughing.

I didn't hear from him until February of 1999 He left a message saying he wanted to discuss something with me. I returned his call and did a total recall of his palm in my mind's eye. I went back in my memory until I saw it. I remembered he wore a black tux with a red brocade vest and matching bow tie. He was stunned I was able to describe his hand.

"I can visualize your palm," I began. "Yours was a forty year marriage and the loss of a spouse. Your second connection appears in the late sixties. This new woman is your soul mate. She lives across the ocean. You will correspond with one another, meet, and then spend many happy hours together. I see her relocating to this area when you will formally date, then become lovers, and eventually you will marry."

"Oh!" he breathed, "You hit the nail on the head! That's exactly what's been happening. She's moving to my hometown this spring. I plan to go to Prague to help her close on the sale of her home and to sell her antique furniture. We'll come back to Boulder together. She's renting a home down the lane from me."

I continued, "This woman is a few years younger than you and has been alone for ten years, since the death of her husband. She's pretty, intelligent, interesting to talk to, plays classical piano beautifully and she's lively. She has good energy and is a kind-hearted person. She liked you immediately from the sound of your letters. The reason you gravitated to one another is due to your similar losses. Between you there is no friction or any kind of manipulation."

"When should we plan to marry?" he inquired.

I answered, "Things fall into place when they are supposed to and when that happens it will be time for a frank discussion. You are in her thoughts and she is in yours. This is a special mental telepathy most don't have. She is intuitive and spiritual, kind, gentle and caring. I see that you are truly a loving, generous, giving man. All of these characteristics meshed together can only make this union magical. It's a win-win situation for both of you."

#32 SOUL MATE WAITING IN THE WINGS: March 1999

I received a telephone call one Saturday afternoon from a woman I met a year earlier. She owned a fitness-clothing store.

"Can you fit me into your schedule? I have an emergency and I need a reading," she said.

"What time do you close the store tonight?" I inquired.

"I'm slipping out at 5:30 today because my son has a Cub Scout POW WOW event I have to attend with him," she answered.

We arranged for a house call reading at 5:00 PM at her store. Upon arriving I noticed the counter had been cleared, a tape recorder set up, and a huge basket of wild flowers parked there.

"Beautiful arrangement," I commented. "Who sent them?"

"My sisters thought I needed cheering up - they sent them," she replied.

I studied her palm and the session began.

"From your low energy level you aren't sleeping well," I began. "I sense fear."

She admitted, "You're right, I'm nervous and not sleeping at all."

"Is your husband giving you a hard time, talking at you constantly, belittling you, giving you this heartache?" I asked. "I feel his hatred and resentment. Does he pick on everything you do?"

She answered, "He's been treating both my son and I brutally, mentally. Marriage is supposed to be a partnership but he never viewed it that way."

"Your palm shows there's no togetherness; you both go your own ways. There is nothing in common here. He's been thinking of leaving for two years; every time he gets involved with another woman he gets angry and takes it out on you and your son. He appears unstable. Do you believe staying in this relationship is healthy for your child?" I questioned.

"I have already filed for divorce. He went crazy last week, had my car repossessed, then went into bankruptcy court and took the house away. I panicked and called friends in the middle of the night; they moved us to my parents' condo north of town. Since they are in Belize for six weeks it was a haven for us. When they return I'll have to get a place of my own."

"Sounds like a terrible predicament to me," I sympathized.

"I'm lonely and needy too," she said.

Their relationship had been falling apart for several years. I noticed the deterioration didn't just happen. I mentioned it and she agreed with me.

"I need advice and I trust your intuition," she began. "A man I was in love with twenty years ago walked into the store last week. We recognized each other and he was genuinely happy to see me. We talked for two hours while I waited on customers. He wants to date right away but I'm fearful of hurting the divorce. If anyone saw me out before it's final, it could ruin things in court."

I studied her Love line. The first marriage of eighteen years would be finished in a few months; it would be painful and hurt like hell, but I knew it would be scheduled. Her hand showed a second union, a soul mate, waiting in the wings until she obtained martial freedom. They were both in their early forties. There was very little time between the end of one union and the beginning of the next on her palm. I knew she would not be alone for long.

"I can picture the man in my mind's eye," I said. "Average height, about 5'10" with a stocky build, maybe a body builder. He has light brown hair worn in an executive style. He wears glasses and he is youthful-looking. How am I doing?" I asked.

"You just described him perfectly," she said.

"I want to explain the soul mate pyramid. "You need to comprehend this information and give it some thought. When the explanation is finished I want you to tell me if he fits the soul mate description. He is with you on numerous levels. There must be trust. Next is expression of thought, communication, verbal or non-verbal in nature. Neither of you will talk down to one another, or tune out when one is talking. You look striking together, like a matched set. He won't look like a grandpa or a young kid, but around your age," I offered.

Listening, she digested the information.

I continued, "You will both be spiritual, compassionate, and know karma exists. You both know there is a universe out there; the vibrations from your energy are going out. A sexual relationship will develop after you are friends, then best friends. It is personal and requires discussion between two consenting adults. Religion is next. It doesn't necessarily mean you have to practice the same religion, but you will both have a similar belief system. Does this person blend with you on all of these levels?" I asked.

Her face lit up like a Christmas tree. Smiling, she replied, "Yes, he sounds exactly like all of that! I can't begin to thank you enough for running down to the store to read my palm in a house call at the last minute. You are valued, a wonderful friend! Your advice is exactly what I needed. I must confess, the basket of flowers arrived with a heart warming card from him."

#33 NOT IN THIS LIFETIME: April 1999

Two women who work at the University of Denver called me for palm reading appointments. They requested sitting in on each other's session. The older of the two women had an interesting hand with numerous lines and feathery markings on it.

I announced, "You are an old soul having traveled this path in three other lifetimes. This is your fourth time on this planet."

"I just knew it!" she exclaimed. "I always knew more than the other kids when I was growing up. At twenty I was more mature and settled than a lot of my girlfriends. I wasn't flighty or an airhead. I always felt competent at work and socially, more self-assured than most."

I replied, "You realized your capabilities at an early age because you've been here previously. You look pretty good for a four hundred year old." I studied her Life line. She was in average health, had a few minor allergies and longevity marked on her palm. Her Love line was excellent. This lady was one in a million for she found, dated and married her soul mate the first time around. They rededicated their love after twenty-five years of marriage in Church with family and friends. A huge celebration followed. She confided the unusual circumstance concerning their twenty-fifth anniversary was the fact their twenty-one year old daughter chose the same date for her wedding in the same Church at the same time.

"Am I ever going to be rich?" she asked jokingly.

"Not in this lifetime," I answered. "Any money you come into will be earned, but I do see early retirement for you."

"You got me 100%," she laughed. "I'm quitting the University this fall when I turn sixty-two. Retirement is only a few months away."

I explained the stripes on her fingers denoted leadership, a person with a lot on the ball who had bright ideas. She was pleased to learn her record of schemes was carried on her palm.

"They all call me Lucy at the University," she volunteered. "My partner in crime is Ethel, here. We come up with hair-brained things to do to liven up the workplace."

I showed her on her palm, that she had a few close friends and many acquaintances. I explained she was a good friend and everyone dumped on her because she was easy to talk to and she didn't tell people how to run their lives. She simply listened.

#34 WHAT DOES THE FUTURE HAVE IN STORE FOR ME?: June 1999

I worked at a beauty salon in Louisville Colorado as a palmist when I met a hairdresser whose unusual energy caught my attention. She asked for a reading before our appointments arrived. We found a quiet corner in the shop and sat down. I studied her petite hand.

"You have many abilities and talents," I offered. "I can see potential you haven't realized yet."

"I'm a master hair designer," she answered.

"On your Work line I note you owned your own business in another state. It feels like an all day SPA, not just a beauty shop. You had pricey fees for massage, tanning, aromatherapy, waxing, and the works. Am I right?" I inquired.

She replied, "Exactly! I had sixteen operators on nine-hour shifts six days a week. It was exhausting working like that, but we had great fun! The shop had marble pillars and floors, fountains, dreamy music, plants and filmy drapes everywhere. Movie stars came in too."

"Why did you leave the glitzy California lifestyle for Colorado," I asked.

She replied, "I relocated when my twenty year old daughter moved here with her fiancée. I only have one child and I wanted to share the good times with them. I had just gotten divorced and it seemed like the place to go. I've never been sorry I left. It's been four years and some of my old clients are still asking for me. I found an old mansion, and rented it very cheaply near downtown Denver. I made friends with a younger woman and we became roommates. Then I met a guy who knocked my socks off. For two years ours was a hot and heavy romance. He's never been married, afraid to commit. I was famously close to his family. In fact I'm still in contact with them. One day I woke up and decided I wasn't getting any younger. If nothing was going to come from our relationship I had to end it. It broke my heart, but I got out. What's in my future?" she asked.

I explained it would take time to heal from the past relationship but she would eventually connect with a wonderful man who would read her moods, wants and needs.

"Sounds like a catch! Where will I meet this wonderful guy?" she questioned. "I hate being alone. I usually find a partner pretty fast."

"Give yourself time to unwind from the last coupling. Take a breather before you latch on to someone new or it will be a rebound, a throwaway romance that will be your next victim. To meet quality people you must be quality yourself. You have to unload old baggage before acquiring new. It's up to you to respond to someone else's needs. He'll be in sad shape from a rotten romantic entanglement he was trapped in for ten years but you'll be there for him when he needs support, a shoulder to lean on. This time you have to be the care-giver, not the taker," I explained.

"I can be the care-giver in a relationship," she offered. "I'm very deep, internalized. I usually don't like needy men. I detest people who talk the talk but don't walk the walk."

"When you're ready this man will appear on the scene," I announced. "He will be physically attracted to you. When he learns who you are and understands where you're coming from the two of you will be inseparable," I predicted.

"Do I already know him? Is he good-looking, well built, and intuitive? Does he have a professional life?" she asked, rapid fire.

I replied, "You have never met him. He is quite handsome, tall, built like a football player, and able to "know" things; he is intuitive. He owns his own business. I must caution you to slow down on man hunting for a while. When your back is turned, and you don't expect it, he will appear. It will be natural," I counseled.

"L", a forty-seven year old woman called for an appointment. "I need advice about my marriage," she announced.

After studying her palm I noticed numerous complications on her Love line. "L" 's dilemma: she married at eighteen and her husband was eleven years older, divorced with the custody of four children. She raised them along with the three they produced. Theirs was a home that was a happy, noisy, place. Nine months earlier her man's behavior suddenly changed. He constantly complained their two youngest children; twenty-three year old twin girls should be out of the house, on their own. Having just graduated from college, they were in the process of sending out resumes. He was weary of having children underfoot.

"L" said, "He's been unhappy for the last nine months and started drinking heavily, not just socially. He's been hard on the family, acting out, disagreeable, nit-picky, and talking to himself loudly."

"L" explained he wanted to quit working, but at age fifty-six knew financially he had to continue. Her salary couldn't sustain the family.

"Are you fearful of his temper?" I asked.

She replied, "Yes, he sometimes gets violent and hits the twins or me. It only happens when he's been drinking and his temper flares."

I asked if he would seek help, guidance. She shook her head 'No'.

"I'm at the end of my rope," she began. "He didn't come home last night so I walked over to the neighborhood bar where he sometimes goes when he works late. I discovered him sitting in the back of the joint in a darkened booth kissing some woman. She was younger than me!" Tears welled in her eyes. "I love that man! I've given him my "all" and raised seven children almost single-handedly. If he did that last night, how about all those other times he was late?" she sobbed.

"Your palm shows you love him almost to a fault, but his love for you and the family isn't what it used to be. He's been out of touch for a while, this predicament's been building for a few years," I explained.

"What can I do Myrna Lou?" she asked, eyes brimming with tears.

I replied, "I would back off. Can you stay in the background? Play it out and allow whatever happens to unfold. You can't change him but you can change yourself. He may get over his weirdness, his mid-life crisis, and be glad you were there for him. He could return to his old happy-go-lucky self, or he may simply continue on the same destructive path. My advice is wait and see."

#36 WHERE IS MY SOUL MATE?: September 1999

A middle-aged Boulder woman called for a palm reading appointment. I checked her reference and we set a time. I noted, "M" was very nervous and agitated when she arrived as she sat down. Immediately she began fidgeting with the straps on her purse, squirming in the chair.

"Are you having "man trouble"?" I asked.

"Yes," she answered. "I called you because I have issues."

I asked her if she was living with anyone.

"Not since two days ago," she sniffed. "I threw him out of my apartment. He had such a hurt look on his face when he left that I'm not sure I did the right thing. Maybe we should make up and get back together."

104

"There must have been a valid reason for you to tell him to leave," I remarked. "I think you should continue along this path. See where it takes you."

"I'm dropping off his clothes and personal stuff tonight," she offered.

"I suggest not going to his place alone. One thing will lead to another and you'll get sucked back into a sick relationship. Do you have a friend who might go with you?" I inquired.

"My girlfriend is going so I won't have to be alone with stupid," she explained.

I studied her Life line and told her she had longevity in her heredity, where it showed she was strong with good genes. She smiled. I explained her Love line was complicated and she agreed.

"I've never married and I'm thirty-eight years old. Do you think there's anything wrong with me?" she asked.

"Maybe you never married because all these relationships I see marked so clearly on your palm were long term affairs with no commitment. Are you particular about who you date, what food you eat and the clothing you buy?" I questioned.

"Yes, I care about all of those things," she replied.

I inquired, "What is it you desire in a lifetime mate?"

She replied, "I thought I knew what I wanted and needed, but I don't know anymore."

I continued as soothingly as possible, "I see your future with a soul mate, an exciting love who will connect with you within a year."

Sitting very still, she quit fidgeting and listened intently.

"Your "Mr. Perfect" is out there, I'm sure of it. He will be like you in appearance, personality and body shape. You will have the same temperament too. You've always been attracted to the bad boys, the "opposites". This time you will find a "like" and it will stick. Once you connect all the opposites you have been involved with over the years will fade from memory. You will have many interests in common. Neither of you will be the leader, for equality is the key to true happiness in any relationship. Both of you will be fair-minded, putting the other person first," I explained.

"M" was upbeat as she thanked me for her reading.

#37 I'M AFRAID TO BE ALONE: October 1999

I received a phone call from a worried black woman. She said she was hopeful a palm reading session and my guidance would help with her problem. We made an appointment. She arrived late, acted nervous and used my powder room.

She began, "I got myself some real big trouble. I hope you can find me a solution. I need desperately to straighten out my life."

I studied her palm. It revealed her husband's behavior was the problem. Married ten years, they had three children, eight, seven and four.

"What's gonna happen to our marriage?" she asked tearfully.

I explained, "This problem isn't brand new, it's been ongoing for quite awhile."

"I know," she said quietly. "My husband and his best friend have recently become very important and close to each other."

Looking at her Love line I noticed a stripe across the wishbone mark, denoting finality, a divorce. I said nothing about it at that time.

"It feels like my soul mate's pushing me and the kids out of his life. I got suspicious about his peculiar habits these last few weeks and I did a bad thing, I tape recorded some of his phone calls," she reported.

I questioned, "What possessed you to tape record his private phone calls?"

"His best friend is this white woman he knows since high school. She's married with five kids. They've always kept in touch, only lately they call back and forth a lot more often," she stated.

"I overheard them planning sneak dates. He told her if she'd get divorced he would too, then they could be together forever. Wouldn't that shake you up?" she cried.

I asked if her husband had any idea she overheard any of his conversations with his lady friend. She shook her head. I asked if she confronted him with the information or the tapes.

"I'm scared to because he'll go violent on me, or hit on the kids," she sobbed.

She said he took her for granted, thought she should run the house, work an eight hour shift at her job, care for the children, be a good wife to him and not bother him. He assumed she was too busy to notice his behavioral change.

"I need my man," she wailed. "I got to hang on to him for the kids sake. They need their Daddy and I'm afraid to be alone!"

I handed her the Kleenex box and asked if she wanted to hold on to someone who didn't want her.

Tears slipped down her worried face and she began to cry really hard. We sat in silence for a few minutes, the tape recorder turned off. When she calmed down she thanked me and left.

#38 AM I TOO PICKY?: April 2000

An Oriental woman called for a palm reading session the day after I participated in a bookstore Psychic Fair. "I must see you ASAP," she said breathlessly. Kevin, a reader at the bookstore fair turned me on about you. He says you're accurate."

We set an appointment and she arrived at my home at the designated time. I noticed she was immaculately groomed and dressed. She carried herself with a stage presence. I explained how I conducted readings, going over the main areas, then the various miscellaneous lines.

"I never had palm reading," she said. "I'm a little nervous but know you will help me."

"Your Love line shows an early marriage lasting ten years. You chose a man who was unlike you in every way. You divorced a few years ago. There are two teenagers at home and you are the sole wage earner," I began.

"You got me!" she said, laughing.

"You're particular about where you go and you are picky about how you look," I explained.

"That's me. I don't want to waste time going out with men who have nothing in common with me. I know I'm a pretty good catch for someone, but most men want sex, or drape me on their arm like a trophy because of how I look," she replied, sadly.

"There's someone in this world for each of us," I said, "I'm a romantic. Relax your standards a bit and you'll find the right man. He will meet your needs and expectations. There are no perfect people, you know."

She listened to me, eyes closed, as if picturing her future mate. She sighed. I remained quiet until she was focused. "I just asked Buddha allow me to relax about dating," she said, smiling, "I will be more human now. Maybe I'll find somebody."

"Have you ever modeled or been in the movies?" I inquired.

She explained she acted in radio and television commercials in China.

"People take advantage and dump on you. Do you provide money and too much of yourself to your family?" I asked.

"I send money home to my parents all the time. When I stop they get nasty, really angry. Sometimes I need money for me and for my children. My kids are both wonderful; my son and girl are just like me. They have good habits, attitudes, and both are particular too. My son irons every single thing he wears; he learned watching me. I hope when they grow up they don't have trouble meeting their soul mate like me," she said.

"You are a compassionate person, kind, easy-going, considerate. I see you work two jobs, long hours. You are responsible at work and pitch in to help others if you see they have a problem keeping up. You're a team player and everyone appreciates you at work," I explained.

She answered, "I am easy-going girl. I was a straight A student in school too. Things come to my mind quickly. If someone is struggling at work, I help. I don't mind."

I began, "You have many interests and you are running to something every day. Sometimes you go out with your girlfriends and sometimes you go out alone. You are trying to fill your off work hours. This is not quality use of your time."

She agreed she kept busy when not at work, finding things to do.

"Why can't I find a good man?" she wailed. "I go many places, I see many men there, but never do I make friends with the right one."

"Shake up your routines and change some of your activities. Do new things alone, and then you will bump into new faces. Stop doing whatever it is you are doing now because you aren't meeting anyone. Turn your attention to a new path, take a class, volunteer, get involved with Church or a singles group or go to a recreation center. Do anything that involves single people," I suggested.

She asked, "Know what I did yesterday? I was out with a realtor who showed me houses with a few acres, barns and properties. Should I invest? I like Elizabeth Colorado a lot."

"I cannot advise you on investing, however, I see a new home being built for you in the mountains by your new mate. If you go east to a farm area you will be moving west the following year, to the foothills. The man you'll fall in love with will be well off financially and have definite ideas of what he wants and where he wants to live with you," I said.

"I'm getting excited already to make acquaintance with him!" she laughed. "Where is he now and how can I meet him?"

I suggested, "Either volunteer in a hospital or facility that needs a hand on Sunday. He's lonely and volunteers then. He is a kind, compassionate man, but he needs a mate. If you go where he is, a match of personalities will be automatic. You will fit together like two puzzle pieces."

"I thank you from the bottom of my heart for helping me understand I need a change," she said.

"I believe your reading was right on. I am impressed. Now I going home to think about where I should go next Sunday. You speak the truth, I run around and accomplish nothing."

She thanked me for her reading and dashed out of my house.

#39   I DON'T WANT TO RAISE TWO CHILDREN: June 2000

I read the hand of a manicurist, unmarried, four months pregnant. She asked for my advice.

"My boyfriend is dumb," she said. "We just broke up and I threw him out of the house because he drinks, does drugs with his friends and wasn't paying any attention to me. Now I sit and cry all the time. What do you see about our relationship?"

I studied her palm. It showed she was a survivor with a strong personality. He was weak. Theirs was an unhealthy union. She was highly organized, detail-oriented, capable in work and running a home. He was a youngish twenty-two and wanted to be mothered. He felt like a seventeen year old to me.

"Myrna Lou," she whispered, "I gave him an ultimatum to grow up and quit behaving like that or he would be out of my life. He chose his friends and habits over me. Now I'm all alone!"

"He's going to rethink this and come back into your life," I said. "But first he needs to get used to the idea of being a father, of giving up his youth and becoming a responsible person."

She thanked me for the advice and left feeling a bit calmer.

Four months passed when I received a phone call from the manicurist. She requested an update reading. When I saw her this time she looked radiant, happy and peaceful.

"I'm here because I want to discuss my life now," she announced. "I'm in the thinking stage and I need a shove. You'll probably make up my mind for me. My boyfriend has been attentive, giving me money for pre-natal meds, attending La Mas class with me, buying groceries, and helping me clean the house. I think this may be an act until the baby arrives. I don't know if I should allow him to move back in with me or not."

I took a deep breath. "He's not all grown up in the last four months simply because you're going to be parents. He is showing affection and partnership and wants to be back in your life, permanently."

"That's how I see it too. Does he want back in so I can be the care giver again?" she questioned. "I will be mothering a newborn, I don't need two children around my neck."

I studied her face to see if she was upset. I began quietly, "It's up to you. If you do decide to take him back you should start over in a new home, a different location. He may or may not slip into his old routines with his friends. In a new house there will be many things that need attention to detail and he will have to help you settle in, hang drapes and the rest."

We hugged each other and she left.

#40 ARE WE REALLY SOUL MATES?: July 2000

A couple living in my neighborhood called for a dual palm reading on a Sunday afternoon. She was a tall, striking thirty-year old woman with a beautiful face. He was average height, ordinary-looking with reddish hair and wore horn-rimmed glasses. I asked if they wanted to hear each other's reading; they answered yes. Holding her palm in mine I discovered she was under a mental strain, but I said nothing. I noted she was creative and commented on it. She said her education was in physical fitness. She gave me her business cards for yoga instructor and the second one for model, actress, and media announcer. I explained she had to make a career decision as time was running out. She agreed. I noted she was terribly lonely even though married.

"Are we soul mates?" she asked.

I studied her Love line mentally picking up that she had three soul mate symbols on her hand. One opportunity was overlooked in her late teens. She didn't recognize the person when he came on the scene. This partner was her second soul mate even though incompatible at this stage in their lives. Her third soul mate was waiting in the wings should she gain her freedom. I remained silent about number three.

She squinted and said, "I can't believe I'm hearing this."

I immediately changed the subject, discussing work, career changes, and movement into higher finances. She listened, but looked troubled. We completed her reading and she thanked me.

I read the husband's hand as he sat in the hot seat. His hand revealed a marriage before the age of twenty with a child coming early in the marriage. A divorce followed and a second union took place in his late twenties to this woman. His parents were raising his daughter because he was not a responsible person. He was and will always be a mama's boy, definitely not a leader. I studied his soul mate markings. He had only one and it was his wife. He laughed when I said he liked to read science fiction and fantasy books. I visualized him in a room full of books. He said they created a library out of their third bedroom. I determined he was successful in his job. He agreed.

"Do you have a specific question you'd like me to answer?" I asked.

He shook his child-like head 'No'. His wife's jaw dropped when she realized he was backing away from reality.

She inquired, "I want to know what's going to happen to us in the coming year?"

I knew instinctively they would split up and live their lives separately but I answered, "Time has a way of smoothing things out. Turn over your problems to the universe, allow the angels to handle them for you. Maybe counseling is a good idea."

They both thanked me for their readings, gathered their belongings and left.

Early the following morning I received a surprising phone call from her. She said, "I know you were holding back yesterday in our session. Please tell me what you saw. What is happening to our marriage?"

"You already know your relationship is in trouble and has been for many months," I replied. "Take some time and see what develops."

"I feel in my heart there's more to this than what you say," she replied. "I'm intuitive and read faces just as you read hands. Your face was a giveaway something's up."

I admitted, "I did keep some information from you. I don't relate everything when the mate is sitting in the room in session because it can start a fight and I end up being the bad guy when it backfires."

"Can I make another appointment?" she inquired. "I need to know exactly what you saw on my hand."

She arrived that afternoon and we talked their situation over for about an hour. I explained the three soul mate markings on her hand. She asked if she already had an eye on a man if he could be the "one".

I answered "No, the markings aren't red, which would register as an immediate time span: NOW. Anyone you have your eye on today is not that person from another lifetime." However soul mates appear, they will not come unless the person is free of an entanglement. The person they approach must be alone. When they hear your inner wailing, the cry for someone to be close to, the need of their long time friend, they answer that feeling in kind. You are lonesome," I stated. "You have no one to talk to at home."

"That's really true," she replied. "He just isn't there for me mentally. He's distracted, in a haze, and escapes with his books. When I try to get close he pushes me away. Our sex life is absolutely terrible. He has this childish notion marriage should be like in the movies. He found out both parties have to work at it all the time but he doesn't want to do his part. He thinks of us as Ken and Barbie and carries me on his arm like a possession. I don't like that, I want an equal, a partner I can discuss things with, but instead I got a stone wall."

I asked if they tried a separation because her hand showed one in the past year.

"Yes, he moved out for five months and got his own apartment, then wormed his way back in. We dated for awhile and before I knew it, he let the apartment go and he was back home," she remarked.

"I can honestly see that your hand carries a divorce on it," I related.

"I thought we were headed in that direction. Is it going to be soon? I need time to get used to the idea," she answered.

I questioned, "Are you self reliant? Can you survive with two part time jobs if you go that route?"

115

"I would have to find a full time job," she admitted. "I can't support myself and stay afloat this way, but I could live off my charge cards."

I suggested, "Get a full time job, not necessarily in your field, and take anything to prove to yourself you can make it. Save every penny you can in a secret bank account. When the timing is right and you feel secure financially, you can file for divorce."

"I have no family but my friends would support me in this action. I'll be isolated," she sighed.

She had two paths she could follow. Either stay in the bad situation and do nothing, or get on with her life by making changes, setting goals, following a plan through to completion. "I would cut my losses before I got in any deeper," I counseled.

"I know it in my heart that you're right. I just really had to hear it verbalized," she said.

She thanked me for the second session in two days, and left.

#41   HE ACTS LIKE A DRILL SARGEANT: December 2000

A middle-aged couple called for a palm reading session. They settled in and I began by reading the lady's hand first. Her husband remained in the room with us.

"We've were married ten years," she said. "We were divorced two years ago, then got back together. Now we're just living together."

I discovered the problem immediately; she was pressuring a remarriage. He wasn't positive it would work since it caused them so much pain when they were committed before.

"We really do love each other," she whispered. "I simply can't reach him on the remarriage deal. We don't agree on child-rearing."

I asked the ages of their children.

She replied, "We have three in our brood, a fifteen year old son, a twelve year old girl and an eight year old boy. The youngest is ours."

I immediately understood the problem as conflict with the children. He wasn't the father of the two oldest and she resented his disciplining them.

"If you held a family meeting to set guidelines and involved the children in the rule making, wouldn't that alleviate some of the problems you're experiencing?" I asked.

He concluded it was sensible to include the two older children in the family discussions. As I noted the wife's out stretched hand I saw a stubborn streak, an inflexible individual. She put up mental walls when I mentioned it. Suddenly her smiling face turned hard. She admitted she wanted things her way or no way, and defended herself by saying hers was the best way anyway.

"Why not continue living together, unmarried?" I questioned.

She answered, "Because he has all the advantages of a union while I have all the disadvantages of marriage. He can leave if he gets tired of being a family member, like last time. I want security; I want to know our relationship is for keeps this time. I want him to really want us. I know he and I are soul mates too."

He sat back, a pensive look on his face.

"He acts like a drill sergeant with the kids, bossing them and it makes them nervous," she offered.

He chimed in, "I do whatever it takes to make them tow the line. Kids need rules and structure, a plan the family sets up and follows."

"Hey," she countered, "I believe this is my turn. You get to talk when your palm is being done."

I asked, "What do you both really want?"

"Him," she answered. "I love this man with all my heart but this deal is driving us apart."

I said, "Love is unconditional, it's total acceptance of a person, 100% of the time. Disciplining children is in the scheme too. You want him but you expect him to butt out where your children are concerned. Unless you reach some kind of agreement that everyone adheres to, there may come a day when he will leave the family because of the dissension. You must realize by demanding he back off in this area that you are putting a qualification on the relationship. It's stress that doesn't have to be there."

"I need to reach an understanding deep within myself that whatever he does about the kids is OK or he's out of our lives," she noted.

I explained life isn't so black and white. She said she couldn't envision a lifestyle that would work for everybody in the child-rearing area. He shook his head sadly.

"I have to figure out my priorities," she announced.

I replied, "Why not rethink the scenario. You want him in your life on a permanent basis so you have to demonstrate the five of you can live in harmony. If, in time it is working smoothly, a remarriage may happen."

She thanked me for my time and grabbed her purse. "I'll wait out in your family room while you read his hand," she said solemnly. "I think you need privacy and I have to think about our finding solutions."

He extended his palm and I studied it. His Love line was red, which meant he was up for it but it showed aggravation and pain. "You love your ex-wife but there are reservations about making it forever," I explained.

"Right. When we were married we nearly killed each other over the children. I don't want to live through that kind of hell again, ever. In order to make rational decisions about a remarriage we have to deal with this issue and resolve it before we can move forward. Living in this environment has my stomach in knots," he offered.

Probing a bit, I asked him if he was angry.

"Darn right I am! Wouldn't you be in this trick bag? I'm skeptical about our union," he answered.

"Can you see a marriage counselor? Perhaps a third party can help set up an amicable system that will work for everybody. The family has to work and play within set boundaries," I suggested.

He replied, "I feel it's a good idea for us to go to mediator too, but she won't go to anyone with or without me. A palm reading session was the only thing she would agree to anyway. She wants the family unit, but she doesn't want to contribute to it or give it any thought or energy. I have to be absolutely convinced that we can survive as a nuclear family unit again before I commit."

I explained, "If you feel trapped neither of you will enjoy the relationship. You must be yourself and do what you need to do. Expression of your own opinions and personalities is important too. You have to be free, and behave normally with each other. You can't change her and she can't change you. I hope if you remarry it will give you both joy, happiness and peace of mind."

He nodded, deep in thought. I stopped talking, respecting his silence. He shook my hand and thanked me for his session, then walked into the adjoining family room and hugged his wife. They wept in each other's arms. When they left my house they were arm in arm.

#42 THE FAN CLUB: January 2001

I was the entertainment for a group on a Sunday afternoon in Littleton Colorado. Everyone was already present when I arrived except the man, "F", who engineered the party.

The doorbell rang. I heard, "Quick, somebody my hands are full!"

It was "F" with a gorgeous, homemade chocolate cake. "Mom made this for our party," he said, "I hope you like it Myrna Lou. She decorated it with a palm and drew the lines on it for you."

I was impressed with her artwork and read every line she drew. "Hurry, someone get a picture of this before we cut into and ruin it," I said. "I've never seen anything like this. Please thank your mother for me."

After lunch we went downstairs to the recreation room where a large table was set up for the palmistry party with my magnifier, lamp and tape recorder. I read everyone's palms out loud at the table in front of the group but "F's. He requested a private reading. The hostess took her cue from him and had all the guests' retreat upstairs while he and I remained downstairs. I studied his lines. "You are nearly forty years of age," I began, "You've had a lot of dating experience but you've never committed to anyone on a long-term basis. Am I right?"

"You are a quick-study," he replied. "I admire your ability, your talent. I have had many women in my life, yet never a lasting involvement with anyone for more than a year."

We touched on his Life line, Work and the Bracelets. He confided he didn't want to end up alone, taking care of his mother for the rest of his life.

He asked, "Am I too finicky? Is that why I haven't found my special woman? Why can't I meet my soul mate? I need an eligible, nice woman in my life forever."

I advised him to get involved in groups either through work, church, or at the local recreational center.

He admitted, "I don't want my friends to know I'm in this desperate situation. I signed up with a dating service but nothing's come of it. I even read those newspaper ads where men seek women. I called a few of them to no avail. Is there something wrong with me?"

I replied, "Your Love line shows a romance forthcoming in a few months. You've connected with several women before, but your mother finds fault with every one of them and tears them down in your eyes. You listen to her instead of your heart. Rely on your own judgement next time. After all, you're a grown man and you don't need her approval. Obsessing on not having a mate doesn't help your situation, so relax and try not to dwell on it. There is someone out there for you. I'm a romantic and believe it will happen."

"Myrna Lou, it's all I think about night and day," he said.

I suggested, "You're afraid you're going to be alone for the rest of your life. I can smell the desperation coming from you. Stop this destructive behavior and your life will change. Why not take a vacation and just let yourself go? Ever hear of Club Med? Or a Cruise for Singles? There are many other options too."

He thanked me for his reading as we walked upstairs.

#43 PLEASE DON'T TELL MY WIFE: April 2001

I was the entertainment performing palm reading at a surprise birthday party held at a small local airfield. The unheated hanger was packed with parked planes, a small jet, several single and twin engines and few vintage models no longer in use, along with several wrecked ones on display. I set up my magnifying lamp on a desk in a dark corner of the building. The birthday girl enjoyed having me there for her guests. She opened her gifts, then everyone ate dinner from a beautifully decorated, catered table. I read her palm first. She was happy to learn about her work promotion, travel and financial gain coming in the chronological year. I read many of the participants hands. The last person in line was the most interesting and intriguing. Married to the sister of the celebrating birthday girl, he was handsome and dynamic. His wife was educated, poised, full of confidence, well rounded and pretty. She could have been a model. They made a lovely couple together. When I studied his hand he politely asked her to leave that section of the hanger. He requested a private palm session.

"I waited for the end of the line to have my reading," he began. "I think you'll discover information about my past that no one here is aware of about me."

I expected to detect a tidbit of information I might discuss with him. He was tense, his face full of fear, but his body language registered calmness. I wondered what secrets were hidden from loved ones and friends. His reading commenced as I began with the Life line. The Love line was complicated, full of relationships and terminated engagements, numerous women dropped by the wayside. I thought to myself that he must have been quite the "playboy" in his youth.

I stated, "There are three marriages clearly marked on your Love line."

He explained, "The first was for less than a year. I was a young nineteen. The second was in my mid twenties and it wasn't good either. We were either hot or cold, with volatile temper flare-ups. That union lasted six years even though we weren't suited to each other. No children were produced thank goodness. I spent the next fifteen years alone, thinking I wasn't marriage material, until I met my wife."

"Why does this information make you so uncomfortable?" I asked.

"Because," he replied, "My wife and her family, thought when she met me four years ago that I was this great catch, a confirmed bachelor. I just never set the record straight, I never let on any different. If they were to discover I lied about my past they'd assume I've been hiding other news from them," he reflected.

I studied his Work line. "You've held many different kinds of jobs in various places and never stick very long," I established. "If you don't like a company, or the people there or things don't go the way you expect them to, you're out of there."

"It happens that way sometimes. If they try to cheat me out of earned commissions, I have no choice but to leave," he confirmed.

I noted he worked at the last job for three years and had been as steady as rain. He enjoyed the people and the salary. I announced he worked in his wife's family business. He nodded in agreement.

I asked, "Where do you see yourself in five years?"

"I knew you'd project on the work situation!" he exclaimed.

"I feel movement away from family, the job and even your mate," I said.

He looked into my eyes and admitted he was getting that restless feeling after four years of being married. He admitted he felt stifled, stressed, held back, and almost suffocated at home. He explained his wife smothered him with too much attention, wouldn't allow him the freedom to do anything unless it included her. He took a deep breath, "I own that jet parked over there. I can chart a course and just go off anytime. The family is great, so close knit and all, but it's not good for me. My wife is the clinging vine type and I'm really unhappy. I go to work and do my day-to-day routines so no one suspects anything. I trust you to be cool when you mix it up with everybody out there. Please don't tell my wife any of this."

I agreed saying whatever came out of a reading was client privilege and that I never repeated it to anyone. He thanked me for his reading.

#44   WE COME FROM TWO DIFFERENT WORLDS: May 2001

A client had her palm read twice in the same month, an unusual occurrence since I only need to read a person's palm once a year. I read her in a double session, as her husband sat in and I also read his hand. She realized I held back information in the session and called me a few days later to schedule another appointment.

On her second visit she asked me if I knew of Sinbad. I responded he was a black entertainer. She acknowledged a crush on him and told me she sent him her headshot from the portfolio she used to obtain work. Because her marriage was nearing completion she needed an escape valve, someone to hang on to until it finalized.

"Did you know Sinbad has a home in Denver?" she asked.

I replied, "No."

"I've dated lots of black men," she offered. "Will my next marriage be with a black man?"

I answered, "Your next marriage, will be to a Caucasian." I advised it was premature to send letters or pictures to men until her divorce was final and she was completely free. They were living under the same roof, however they were not having relations. I explained silly indiscretions might ruin her chance for a sizable settlement. A few days later I went to the Post Office to pick up my mail when I discovered a letter from her. This is its exact contents:

Dear Myrna Lou,

Thank you for your guidance and help! Below is a detailed description listing what I believe my soul mate (husband) will be like:

He will be 6'2", between the ages of 35 and 40.

He will be fit and healthy, and a vegetarian.

There will be no children from previous marriages or relationships.

He will be emotionally secure, a responsible person.

He will have a low sexual drive, but be romantic, passionate about life.

He will love exercise and yoga.

He will like the entertainment industry.

He will love animals.

He will possess a wide range of emotions.

He will live in Colorado.

He will be a goal-setter.

He will be financially well off, with earnings of $55K annually.

He will desire growth in personal relationships.

He will be highly involved with life.

He will enjoy making others laugh, be upbeat, a happy individual.

I seek your opinion. Are these realistic expectations? Can you visualize me connecting with this dream man?

I did not acknowledge the letter, or react. It appeared sophomoric to me. I know once she follows through with the divorce she will need time to grieve the lost relationship. Even though they live together, neither is happy. They are from two different worlds and do not understand or have feelings for one another. She is practical, smart and sharp in appearance, enterprising and a hard working person. He is a dreamer, never plans anything, has no ambition, is average looking, lazy with a poor work ethic.

I stated her future was bright and that one day she would feel secure, strong. I explained the lines on her hand represented many talents, abilities and potential, unrealized. When she is back on firm footing she will be ready and able to accept and give love to another. When the day Mr. Right arrives in her life they will connect on many levels. She is a survivor.

#45 CHANGE IS GOOD: April 2001

Standing at my front door one Saturday at noon, was a former co-employee who asked if I would read her palm. We went downstairs to the room where I hold sessions. She brought me up to date on her life since we hadn't seen each other in two years. She was in a state of agitation, having just broken off her current relationship the evening before. I studied her palm. She had developed new lines on her palm, illustrating growth and flexibility since I had last read her hand. It showed movement away from the present romantic situation.

126

"You've been involved in work, with new friends and with a man. I feel tension and relief. Are you happy with the decision to break it off? Is your job driving you nuts? Why did you suddenly pop up on the spur of the moment when we haven't talked in all this time?" I asked.

Twisting in her seat, she began, "I knew in my heart this guy wasn't for me, but he was better than no date. He was abused as a child and is fearful of everything. He would say 'be careful when you drive in snow', or 'keep a watch out for men following your car on the way home' all the time. I wanted to scream sometimes, but I never admitted to him that I didn't like his constant mothering me. I want to meet a variety of normal men with all types of personalities. I want someone who wants me as much as I want him. Montessori school finally got to me too. I wanted it badly when I joined the staff, but now I realize teaching isn't what I truly want. Your name popped into my head - I remembered you always straightened me out if I got in a pickle. It felt logical that you would guide me on the right path."

I listened and came up with a feasible plan. My reply surprised her. "Why not take a vacation, get your feet wet on foreign soil and relax on spring break. Once you leave familiar surroundings you'll appreciate the whole picture more clearly and you'll have a different perspective on some of your issues when you return," I suggested.

"I'd love to take my son and just go!" she answered, enthused. "Maybe I can locate reservations somewhere today. It is late to begin planning for two weeks away though, darn it."

I said, "In your heart you know this man isn't going to just walk out of your life. He listened to your explanation last night and left. After he has time to think it through he'll fight the break-up. He'll make up excuses to call or simply drop by to keep in touch. He may stalk you on dates, or follow you home or show up at work. Be alert, prepared for erratic, lovesick teenage behavior on his part."

She sobbed, "I was afraid of that. What will I do? If he bothers me I'll never get to go out."

"That's why I'm suggesting a vacation for you and your son. It would soften the blow of the relationship ending if you were out of sight. He would have no choice but to simmer down. By leaving town you'll be out of harm's way," I explained. "Your ideals about work have not been realized. You thought the Montessori teaching assignment would give you the feeling of satisfaction you so desire, but there has been no joy in it. You think of the students as spoiled rich kids with maids who don't care if they learn or not. Right?" I asked.

"I feel like that school is a dark pit and I have to enter it everyday and feed the animals. I must finish the school year because I signed a contract. I make a commitment and I honor it. I'm not the little, old schoolteacher after all," she admitted.

I answered, "When the term is over hand in your resignation. The staff will be amazed by your actions but will allow you to leave gracefully, with no fanfare. Over the summer you can plot a new career move. Your Work line is full of movement and activity. You won't leave this area or remove your son from his high school either."

She stared at me in disbelief, eyes opened wide, mouth open. "How do you get all that? Can you see a new man in my future? How will I know if he's my soul mate, the right person for me?" she inquired.

"You'll know because your insides will be screaming it's old home week, a reunion!" I explained. "When you connect with a person from another lifetime, they are not a mystery to you. He will feel the identical pangs of "I know" inside. When you meet it will seem like a miracle. You will be razzle-dazzled by each other. Your feet will not touch the floor when you walk. He will be your true soul mate, with likes and dislikes similar to yours, with attitude, personality, and goal-setting for the future," I said. "The men you've dated were educated, in their forties but none of them had what you needed," I said.

"I don't waste time with anyone who doesn't fulfill my needs and expectations," she replied.

#46 WHAT IF?: May 2001

At the Boulder Creek Festival in Colorado, I conducted palm reading sessions in my tent when a former client and I became reacquainted. She had a reading with me at a fair four years earlier in Littleton Colorado.

She announced, "I got divorced just as you predicted at age thirty-five. Last month I moved to Boulder and began a new job, a new life. I was making new contacts when something awful happened I want to share with you. I avoided tragedy by the skin of my teeth."

Curious, I asked, "What happened?"

"I met this twenty-nine year old guy in a bar. We dated a few times and then he invited me to his cabin in the mountains. I said I'd love to see it. He took me to his hideout in the woods. He had filled my head with visions of great hiking trails, a picnic, saying we'd make a day of it," she said.

As she recounted that day her face grew tense and her eyes clouded. "The cabin he described was only a gutted-out log house. The only thing in there was a dilapidated desk and a chair on wheels in the middle of the front room. I'm not sure what I expected. but I hid my disappointment from him," she reported.

She described the filthy cabin, the dirt road leading up to it from the main paved road, his battered pickup truck, the yard surrounding the cabin and the smell of rotten eggs in the air. She continued, "This guy bragged he brings all his dates to his hideaway in the mountains eventually. He produced ropes he said he used to tie them to the desk chair, then proceeded to explain the game he played where he twirled the women around and around until they were dizzy, crying out, half sick. He said he always got his way sexually because he wouldn't release them until they gave in. He complained it sometimes took hours to make some of them comply, but he never gave them the benefit of the doubt. He said he just kept circling the chair around until they screamed for mercy."

"That guy sounds dangerous to me," I offered.

"You haven't heard the worst part yet," she replied. "He went into a room in the back of the cabin and came back with a long-handled, rusty hatchet covered with blood and long hair hanging off of it. His exact words were, 'If a woman don't cooperate after the chair ride I use this on her.'

I was chilled. "My G-d! What did you do then?"

"I ducked out of the cabin real fast! I ran to the truck and memorized the license plate number. He flew out of the cabin behind me and in an instant grabbed both of my arms, pinning them behind me. I cried out in pain and he got this sorry look on his face. He apologized, and said he didn't mean to scare me. He was playing head games and wanted to see me squirm," she reported.

"My mind was racing. I had to have a feasible plan, fast. I said I forgot I was supposed to be at Community Hospital in Boulder for an orientation with seven doctors for my new job in one hour. He bought the story! We climbed into his truck and headed down the mountain. He dropped me off at the front door of the hospital. I thanked him for the date and walked into the lobby with a purposeful stride. Once safe inside, feeling a bit shaky, I hurried to the nearest pay phone and called the police. They told me until an actual crime was committed their hands were tied. They realized I was threatened, but said since he didn't attack me, in essence I should forget it."

Three days later hikers discovered a young woman's body in Gilpin County Colorado lying on the road just outside a tunnel entrance. Her face and back hacked by a large blade. My client related she heard the report on the noon news and immediately ran to the police department.

"Officer," she began, "I called three days ago about a threat on my life and was told no crime had been committed. Now a murder has taken place and I believe I know the person responsible for it. Who' s going to take my statement around here?"

She told me the police grilled her for three hours. Finally they believed her when she gave them a detailed description of the road, house, yard and odor in the area. She mentioned the ropes and condition of the hatchet. The lead officer asked her to take them to the burned-out cabin. She complied. Upon arriving at the cabin they discovered the desk chair upended, ropes scattered everywhere. The hatchet was on the floor with fresh blood on it, bits of clothing caught in the blade. Fingerprints were lifted and the area surrounding the house searched for fresh graves. The man's prints were the only ones found on the hatchet. An All Points Bulletin was sent out.

"What a nightmare!" I whispered.

"His pickup was spotted by a police cruiser in the parking lot at the base of the waterfall on Canyon in Boulder. The man was wading in the water, washing his clothes. He was taken into custody," she recounted.

"I'm scared to death Myrna Lou! This whole incident has shaken me! I'm leaving town, changing back to my maiden name, and starting over. I'm in the midst of packing boxes now. I knew you'd be at the Festival and I needed to touch base with you so I could share this story."

131

TESTIMONIAL LETTERS

Myrna Lou Goldbaum has frequently offered her "Intro to Palmistry" class at my bookstore, Nic Nac Nook. Well attended, they prove to be fun and enjoyment for the audience. Her palm readings are always a huge success. I've found her to be professional, representing herself well making a most favorable impression on all my customers.

Candie Tsuchiya,
Owner Nic Nac Nook Books, Denver CO

Myrna Lou had the phones ringing as my guest on the "Lights ON" radio show. She generated enthusiasm and audience participation. Her professional explanations removed the visual obstacles of radio and were easily understood.

Nancy Lee,
Producer, Host of "Lights ON with Nancy Lee"
Ft. Collins CO

Not only is Myrna Lou an accomplished palmist, she is a down-to-earth person. There is nothing false about her. What you see is exactly what you get! I truly enjoyed my session with her. She described the elements of my personality and seemed to sense my soul. Her reading was exactly what I needed at the time.

Barbara Bianco, New Age Guide About.com, Denver CO

I have known Myrna Lou Goldbaum for over five years. She is a remarkable, dedicated palm reader, and is one of the most diligent, successful professionals I have ever been fortunate to work with in my career. She will make her book a best seller because that is who she is and she will not rest until the job is done.

Kelley Rosano, Speaker, Author, Astrologer, Boulder CO

Myrna Lou is a gifted, spirited and accurate palm reader. She has been a guest on my TV show, Patrisha: Mystical Insights five times. Almost no one is invited back that many times to be a guest on this show unless they are really exceptional.

Patrisha Richardson, Television Producer/Host, Denver CO

As a Corporate Event Planner, my clients depend on me to provide vendors that are reliable, professional and entertaining to a wide array of guests at their events. When a theme party or meeting allows the opportunity to incorporate the amazing feats of palm readers and psychics, Myrna Lou is the first person I call. With her accurate readings and insightful discussion, guests are thrilled to sit down with her. Having worked with Myrna over the past few years at large company events and galas, the responses I receive about her readings are always positive. Her customers are filled with awe at her ability to read their personalities and their projections into the future. Myrna Lou is a true talent with great stories to tell.

Janet Raydon, Director Operations,
Event Design & Production, Boulder CO

Dear Myrna Lou,

Thank you for all your hard work. I have received a lot of compliments on your palm readings. The only problem I'm having is that everyone wants to keep you into overtime! That's a good problem to have . . . I'm looking forward to our bookings this year. The fact you are willing to travel, are on time, very professional and so good with our guests makes my job easier.

Marne Wills Cuellar, Owner,
Marne Interactive Productions, Lakewood CO

Myrna Lou' s knowledge of soul mate relationships had a profound effect on my life. I now attract positive people into my life and have become more aware of those who might influence me negatively. Unique in her ability, willingness and sharing she teaches her knowledge of palmistry to others.

Her purpose is to guide individuals to become the best they can be, to develop their full potential for love, happiness and prosperity. She is a truly inspirational palm reader. She jump started my personal growth and renewal by helping me discover my hidden talents and creativity. Helping me overcome unproductive thinking, she encouraged me to focus on my goals for a successful future and how to realize opportunities I never knew existed.

Linda Hilton, Director,
Events & Adventures Denver CO

Myrna Lou Goldbaum is an exceptionally gifted individual! Her insight is invaluable! I find Myrna to be highly entertaining, and a very warm, caring human being. She is truly a "gift from God", and meant to be shared. I thank her from the bottom of heart for everything. She is truly awesome and I keep her in my prayers.

Tina Harrison, Public Relations Director
Colorado Springs CO